# ASCENSION

*A Journey Beyond Space & Time*

# ASCENSION

## A JOURNEY BEYOND SPACE AND TIME

*Shaykh*
ABDUL SAMAD AL-QADIRI

TheSunniWay

*Ascension: A Journey Beyond Space & Time*,
SHAYKH ABDUL SAMAD AL-QADIRI

Published by
THESUNNIWAY, PRESTON
THESUNNIWAY.COM

ISBN: 978-1-957773-08-7



*Version 1.1,* Rajab 1444 | February 2023
Printed January 2025

# Contents

# Publisher's Note

MUFTI ZAHID HUSSAIN

ALLĀH'S NAME TO BEGIN WITH, THE MOST COMPASSIONATE, THE EVER-MERCIFUL.
*May His blessings always be upon the Best of Creation and Messengers.*

The following is a much-needed original work developed by the *Khalīfah* of Qā'id al-Millah Muftī `Asjad Riḍā' in the USA, Mawlānā Sayyid `Abdul Ṣamad on the topic of *'Isrā'* and *Mi`rāj*. It has been brought to you by TheSunniWay, an organization of the *'Ahl al-Sunnah* propagating the path of Sayyidī 'A`lā Ḥaḍrat 'Imām 'Aḥmad Riḍā رضي الله عنه. This work will not only educate our *Sunnī* community of the Beloved's ﷺ *sīrah*; rather, it will deepen the roots of the very creed of 'Islām within our hearts.

May Allāh accept this effort and reward Mawlānā Sayyid `Abdul Ṣamad and the entire organization immensely, and grant prosperity in this world and the next to them and their families. I pray that they remain steadfast upon the path of Sayyidī 'A`lā Ḥaḍrat رَضِيَ ٱللَّٰهُ عَنْهُ and keep spreading his light throughout the globe untouched of the evils of the jealous and ill-willed.

ZĀHID HUSSAIN AL-QĀDIRĪ,
*may he be pardoned.*
*TheSunniWay*
PRESTON, UK
Monday, February 14th, 2023 AD

# Foreword

MUFTI FAIZAN UL-MUSTAFA

ALLĀH'S NAME TO BEGIN WITH, THE MOST COMPASSIONATE, THE EVER-MERCIFUL.
*We praise Allāh and send blessings upon His noble messenger.*

The journey of *Mi`rāj* is a grand miracle of his sanctified eminence صَلَّى ٱللَّٰهُ عَلَيْهِ وَسَلَّمَ. Rather, it is a conjunction of unnumbered miracles. Its point of commence is the miraculous journey from *Makkah Mukarramah* to *Bayt al-Maqdis*. Its peak is the viewing of Allāh which Allāh سُبْحَانَهُ وَتَعَالَىٰ granted only to His sanctified beloved صَلَّى ٱللَّٰهُ عَلَيْهِ وَسَلَّمَ out of His own magnanimity. The result was received by us followers in the form of *ṣalāh*, which is the composite of every form of worship. Allāh سُبْحَانَهُ وَتَعَالَىٰ made this journey of *Mi`rāj* a means of test for the people as such affairs occurred in it that the human intellect cannot even fathom that such an occurrence could take place.

For example, to travel extremely lengthy distances in a brief period of time, to pass through the various layers of the atmosphere in the physical body, to exceed beyond the skies, then to surpass the boundaries of this world journeying to *Lā Makān*, touring heaven and hell, and seeing Allāh سُبۡحَانَهُۥ وَتَعَالَىٰ. All of this is out of the ordinary. Therefore, whoever accepts all of these affairs keeping in sight the power of Allāh, he will be deemed fortunate in the world and hereafter. The amaurotic, those living in doubts and skepticisms, by its partial or complete denial, become underprivileged and deprived. We, the *'Ahl al-Sunnah*, especially those who bear love for the *'Imām* of the *'Ahl al-Sunnah*, the *Mujaddid* of the *Dīn* and *Millah*, 'Imām 'Aḥmad Riḍā', may the Dominant sanctify his secret, have received the extraordinary bounty of Allāh that we completely believe in all of the details of this journey which have been mentioned in the *Qur'ān*, *Ḥadīth*, and that which has been detailed in the books of our predecessors.

Every year when the month of *Rajab Sharīf* arrives, some skeptics begin posing objections on the details of the journey of *Mi`rāj* and attempt to make our gullible people doubtful. Thus, it was necessary that the details of *Mi`rāj Sharīf*, based on authentic narrations, be compiled so that people can be delivered necessary information in an easy-to-understand fashion in English and so that people can take benefit by it and solidify their faith and belief.

My upright student, the honorable, Mawlānā Sayyid `Abdul Ṣamad, may Allāh, the Exalted, protect him, is worthy of laudation that Allāh سُبۡحَانَهُۥ وَتَعَالَىٰ selected him for this task. May Allāh grant him reward for this. It is the dream of this destitute that my students residing in North America offer remarkable services to the religion and fulfill the duties of portraying the accurate image of 'A`lā Ḥaḍrat's path.

All praise is for Allāh, the way these scholars are working in all three fields of oration, writing, and teaching, many of my expectations have become attached to these honorable individuals. *'In Shā Allāh*, Allāh سُبْحَانَهُ وَتَعَالَىٰ will take great services from these honorable individuals and will also grant them the honor of acceptance.

وما هو على الله بعزيز ومنه التوفيق

*It is not overwhelming for Allāh*
*and opportunity is from Him.*

FAQĪR FAIZĀN UL-MUṢṬAFĀ AL-QĀDIRĪ,
*may he be pardoned.*
*Jāmi`ah 'Imām 'A`ẓam 'Abū Ḥanīfah*
*& Tāj al-Sharī`ah Islamic Institute*
LUCKNOW, INDIA
Thursday, January 5th, 2023 AD

# Endorsement

## SHAYKH SAYYID ZAMAN ALI JAFRI

ALL PRAISE IS FOR ALLĀH, THE LORD OF ALL CREATIONS.
*Blessing and salutation upon you, O Seal of All Prophets* ﷺ.

Furthermore, it is of immense joy that my son-in-law, *Ṣāḥibzādah* Mawlānā Sayyid `Abdul Ṣamad 'Akhtar al-Qādirī, may Allāh preserve him, has attained the fortune of praising in prose the creedal, spiritual, rational, and traditional aspects of the grand miracle of the one who traveled to *Lā Makān*, the groom of the night of *'Isrā'*, the spotlight of an assembly in paradise, the one crowned by the seal of prophethood ﷺ, in light of the explanations and clarifications of the seniors and predecessors.

Today, is a time wherein the adversaries of *'Islām*, especially the orientalists, utter nonsense regarding the rational and practical aspects of this miracle. Moreover, the actual sorrow is that the majority of the Muslims, who are uneducated from the religious standpoint and imperfect of faith, become impressed either by the temporary success of the west or their worldly rational arguments and become extremely confused, leading them to doubts and unclarity regarding this miracle of grand stature. In such a time, this attempt is not only an effective response to the doubts and objections, but it is a pillar and an asset for the foundation and protection of faith.

May Allāh, the Ever-Noble, for the sake of the most intelligent, the Beloved ﷺ, make this effort of the young scholar, Mawlānā Sayyid `Abdul Ṣamad 'Akhtar al-Qādirī, may Allāh protect him, beneficial and accepted. May he deliver the benefits of his existence, his knowledge, and his capabilities to the Muslim nation.

آمين بجاه النبي الأمين

*'Āmīn, for the sake of the Trusted Prophet* ﷺ.

Praying and expecting prayers,

FAQĪR 'AKHTAR AL-QĀDIRĪ
SAYYID ZAMĀN `ALĪ JA`FRĪ,
*may he and his parents be pardoned.*
Sunday, *Jamādī al-Thānī* 15th, 1444 AH

# Preface

Of all the creations of Allāh سُبْحَانَهُوَتَعَالَىٰ, the creation He favored most and granted the highest rank to is His Beloved Messenger, the Master of all creations, Sayyidunā Muḥammad صَلَّىٱللَّهُعَلَيْهِوَسَلَّمَ. Though man can see the virtue and excellence granted to him by Allāh سُبْحَانَهُوَتَعَالَىٰ in the fact that Allāh سُبْحَانَهُوَتَعَالَىٰ created him as a perfect being who bears no flaw, Allāh سُبْحَانَهُوَتَعَالَىٰ has granted him miracles that are unmatched even amongst the entire congregation of Messengers عَلَيْهِمُٱلسَّلَامُ.

Amongst the miracles and virtues bestowed unto Sayyidunā Rasūl Allāh صَلَّىٱللَّهُعَلَيْهِوَسَلَّمَ, one will find the miracle of *'Isrā'* and *Mi`rāj*. This was a night in which Allāh سُبْحَانَهُوَتَعَالَىٰ granted His Beloved Messenger صَلَّىٱللَّهُعَلَيْهِوَسَلَّمَ the virtues that many may find impossible to believe. But the true believers submit their faith to Allāh سُبْحَانَهُوَتَعَالَىٰ and understand that Allāh's سُبْحَانَهُوَتَعَالَىٰ divine power cannot be measured; Allāh سُبْحَانَهُوَتَعَالَىٰ is the One who took His Beloved on this miraculous journey, and it is He who made this possible.

This concise work is written with the aim to educate the masses on this miracle of *Mi`rāj* and relay the beliefs expressed by the pious predecessors in this regard.

This work includes verses of the Noble *Qur'ān*, prophetic narrations and numerous statements of scholars explaining this miraculous journey. This work also includes a complete summary of a pamphlet penned by Shaykh al-'Islām A`lā Ḥaḍrat 'Imām 'Aḥmad Riḍā' al-Baraylawī رَضِيَ اللّٰهُ عَنْهُ, named *Munabbih al-Munyah li Wuṣūl al-Ḥabīb 'ilā al-`Arsh wa al-Ru'yah.* This summary has been split into two parts and mentioned in this book according to where it was most appropriate.

I ask Allāh to accept this work and grant showers of blessings in the lives of all those who assisted me in this task; namely my honorable brothers Mawlānā Sayyid 'Asad al-Qādirī and Mawlānā Salmān al-Nūrī, and those students of mine who assisted in its proofreading.

A HUMBLE SERVANT OF `ULAMĀ'
FAQĪR `ABDUL ṢAMAD AL-QĀDIRĪ,
*may he be pardoned.*
Wednesday, January 4th, 2023 AD

CHAPTER ONE

# The Night of 'Isrā' in The Qur'ān

Regarding this night of *'Isrā'*, Allāh سُبْحَانَهُ وَتَعَالَىٰ has stated:

سُبْحَـٰنَ ٱلَّذِيٓ أَسْرَىٰ بِعَبْدِهِۦ لَيْلًا مِّنَ ٱلْمَسْجِدِ ٱلْحَرَامِ إِلَى ٱلْمَسْجِدِ ٱلْأَقْصَا

ٱلَّذِي بَـٰرَكْنَا حَوْلَهُۥ لِنُرِيَهُۥ مِنْ ءَايَـٰتِنَآ إِنَّهُۥ هُوَ ٱلسَّمِيعُ ٱلْبَصِيرُ

*Exalted is the One who took His servant by night from Masjid Ḥarām to Masjid 'Aqṣā, whose surroundings We blessed, to show him some of Our great signs. Indeed, He hears, sees.*[1]

[1] *Sūrah al-'Isrā': 1*

## THE WORD "SUBḤĀN"

In this verse, Allāh سُبْحَانَهُ وَتَعَالَىٰ attributes this miracle of *'Isrā'* to Himself as He سُبْحَانَهُ وَتَعَالَىٰ states, "*Exalted is the One who...*" The Arabic word used here is "*subḥān.*" One meaning of this word "*subḥān*" is to be far beyond, transcendent, or pure of something. There is much wisdom in the use of this word here because the occurrences in the night of *'Isrā'* seemed to be unbelievable to many. Not only was this occurrence a means for the non-believers to ridicule the ones who believed in this miracle, it also caused a few believers to leave the religion of *'Islām.* By mentioning His transcendence, Allāh سُبْحَانَهُ وَتَعَالَىٰ reminds the believers that He is far beyond any weakness, and it was He who made such a miraculous and astonishing journey possible.

'Imām Shihāb al-Dīn al-Khifājī al-Ḥanafī رَحِمَهُ ٱللَّٰهُ mentions that when the occurrences of *'Isrā'* and Sayyidunā Rasūl Allāh صَلَّى ٱللَّٰهُ عَلَيْهِ وَسَلَّمَ seeing Allāh سُبْحَانَهُ وَتَعَالَىٰ were mentioned, it could have caused the listener to assume that Allāh سُبْحَانَهُ وَتَعَالَىٰ is in a particular direction. However, the use of this word proved His transcendence from space and direction. He further mentions that when people belied the Beloved Messenger in this matter, the use of this word showed that Allāh سُبْحَانَهُ وَتَعَالَىٰ is far beyond and free from lying.[2]

[2] *Nasīm al-Riyāḍ: Volume 3, Chapter Regarding the Miracle of 'Isrā'*

## THE WORD "`ABD"

In this verse, Allāh سُبْحَانَهُ وَتَعَالَىٰ stated that the one He took on this journey was His servant. According to 'Imām Fakhr al-Dīn al-Rāzī رَحِمَهُ ٱللَّٰهُ, there is a consensus of all exegetes of the Qur'ān that this word is used here in reference to the Beloved Messenger Sayyidunā Muḥammad صَلَّى ٱللَّٰهُ عَلَيْهِ وَسَلَّمَ.[3]

This night of *'Isrā'* being bestowed upon the most honorable of Allāh's creation was the mark of a distinct rank that had not been granted to anyone previously. However, when Allāh سُبْحَانَهُ وَتَعَالَىٰ is describing this event and the Noble Messenger who was granted such an unmatched favor, Allāh سُبْحَانَهُ وَتَعَالَىٰ describes him as His servant. There are many titles that could have been used to describe Sayyidunā Muḥammad صَلَّى ٱللَّٰهُ عَلَيْهِ وَسَلَّمَ. Sayyidunā Muḥammad صَلَّى ٱللَّٰهُ عَلَيْهِ وَسَلَّمَ is not only a servant of Allāh سُبْحَانَهُ وَتَعَالَىٰ, but he is the Messenger of Allāh, the Prophet of Allāh, the Beloved of Allāh, and the Master of Allāh's Creations. Despite the many titles and words of praise that could have been used to describe him, Allāh سُبْحَانَهُ وَتَعَالَىٰ referred to him as His servant.

A reason as to why Allāh سُبْحَانَهُ وَتَعَالَىٰ referred to Sayyidunā Muḥammad صَلَّى ٱللَّٰهُ عَلَيْهِ وَسَلَّمَ as His servant in this instance could be that though being a general servant is looked down upon, being a servant of Allāh سُبْحَانَهُ وَتَعَالَىٰ is an honor like no other. Any rank granted by Allāh سُبْحَانَهُ وَتَعَالَىٰ to anyone has only been attained after taking on the role of slavery to Allāh سُبْحَانَهُ وَتَعَالَىٰ and thus, every believer wishes to be a slave of Allāh سُبْحَانَهُ وَتَعَالَىٰ and refers to themselves as such. Here, it can be seen that whereas every

---

[3] *Mafātīḥ al-Ghayb, al-Tafsīr al-Kabīr: al-'Isrā': 1*

believer claims to be a servant of Allāh سُبْحَانَهُ وَتَعَالَىٰ, Allāh سُبْحَانَهُ وَتَعَالَىٰ Himself is verifying the claim of Sayyidunā Muḥammad صَلَّى ٱللَّهُ عَلَيْهِ وَسَلَّمَ and is showing that the servanthood which is accepted and recognized in His court is the servanthood of His most Beloved Messenger صَلَّى ٱللَّهُ عَلَيْهِ وَسَلَّمَ. Verily, every servant of Allāh سُبْحَانَهُ وَتَعَالَىٰ who makes the claim of His servanthood desires confirmation from the court of Allāh سُبْحَانَهُ وَتَعَالَىٰ and such was the wish of Sayyidunā Rasūl Allāh صَلَّى ٱللَّهُ عَلَيْهِ وَسَلَّمَ.

'Imām Fakhr al-Dīn al-Rāzī رَحِمَهُ ٱللَّهُ mentions that when Sayyidunā Rasūl Allāh صَلَّى ٱللَّهُ عَلَيْهِ وَسَلَّمَ reached a lofty station in the *Mi`rāj*, Allāh سُبْحَانَهُ وَتَعَالَىٰ asked:

يا محمد بم أشرفك

*"O Muḥammad, how shall I honor you?"*

Sayyidunā Rasūl Allāh صَلَّى ٱللَّهُ عَلَيْهِ وَسَلَّمَ expressed his wish by saying:

رب بأن تنسبني إلى نفسك بالعبودية

*"My Lord, that you attribute me to Yourself by servanthood."*

Allāh سُبْحَانَهُ وَتَعَالَىٰ fulfilled this wish and therefore referred to His Beloved Messenger صَلَّى ٱللَّهُ عَلَيْهِ وَسَلَّمَ as His servant whilst describing this night.[4]

[4] *ibid*

## THE WORDS "'ASRĀ" AND "LAYLAN"

In this verse, Allāh سُبْحَانَهُۥ وَتَعَالَىٰ uses two words to indicate that this journey was one that took place in the night. The first word used which denotes this meaning is the word "*'asrā*." "*'Asrā*" is a word that comes from the root *'isrā'* and is specifically used for journeys that take place in the night.

Further into the verse, the word "*laylan*" is used which again describes the setting and literally translates to "in the night."

Though the use of both words in description of the setting may seem to be a form of repetition, the reality is that the use of the word "*laylan*" after having established that the journey took place in the night only enhances the beauty and the magnificence of this miraculous journey. The word "*laylan*," when used here, is used as a common noun as opposed to a proper noun which would be written as "*al-layl*." The use of the common noun form informs the addressed that this journey was not one that went on for the entire night, but it was one that took place in a very brief period of the night. A journey from the blessed *Masjid Ḥarām* in the city of *Makkah Mukarramah* to *Masjid 'Aqṣā* in the time this event took place would take 40 nights.[5] The Almighty Allāh سُبْحَانَهُۥ وَتَعَالَىٰ, however, took His Messenger صَلَّى ٱللَّٰهُ عَلَيْهِ وَسَلَّمَ not only to *Masjid 'Aqṣā*, but far beyond it and He made this journey possible not only in the time of one night, but in a brief portion of the night.

---

[5] *ibid*

## INDEED, HE HEARS, SEES

In the conclusion of this verse, Allāh states, "*Indeed, He hears, sees.*" But it is unclear as to whom this pronoun is referring to.

According to Shaykh Shihāb al-Dīn al-Khifājī رَحِمَهُ ٱللَّهُ, this pronoun is used here in reference to Allāh سُبْحَانَهُۥ وَتَعَالَىٰ Himself to indicate that He hears all that is said regarding Him, and He sees too. However, the notable scholar also mentions that there is a view which states that this pronoun is used here in reference to the Messenger صَلَّى ٱللَّهُ عَلَيْهِ وَسَلَّمَ and denotes that he, on this journey, will hear the Divine Word of Allāh سُبْحَانَهُۥ وَتَعَالَىٰ and he will see His signs.[6]

---

[6] *Nasīm al-Riyāḍ: Volume 3, Chapter Regarding the Miracle of 'Isrā'*

CHAPTER TWO

# 'Isrā' & Mi`rāj in the Ḥadīth

The details pertaining to the occurrences in the night of *Mi`rāj* are found across several *'aḥādīth*[7] from various narrators. A few of these narrations in this regard will be mentioned with commentary to get an overlook of the events that unfolded on this night.

[7] *'Aḥādīth (pl. of Ḥadīth): Prophetic narrations*

## THE BEGINNING OF THE JOURNEY

Description of how this miraculous journey commenced is found in the narration of Sayyidunā 'Abū Dharr al-Ghifārī رَضِيَ اللَّهُ عَنْهُ. It is narrated from him that the Messenger of Allāh صَلَّى اللَّهُ عَلَيْهِ وَسَلَّمَ states:[8]

فرج سقف بيتي فنزل جبريل ففرج صدري ثم غسله من ماء زمزم ثم جاء بطست من ذهب ممتلئ حكمة وإيمانا فأفرغها في صدري ثم أطبقه ثم أخذ بيدي فعرج بنا إلى السماء...

*"The roof of my house was parted and Jibrīl descended. Then, he split my chest and washed it with water of Zamzam. Then, he brought a basin of gold filled with wisdom and faith. He poured it into my chest then sealed it. Then, he took my hand and raised us to the sky…"*

The narration then continues to mention the remainder of the journey.

In the beginning of the journey, it is seen that instead of seeking permission to enter from the door, Sayyidunā Jibrīl عَلَيْهِ السَّلَامُ enters through the roof.

A possible reason for such an entrance is mentioned by 'Ibn al-Munīr.[9] According to him, this was a form of increasing the element of surprise and unlikelihood of this journey. This was highlighting the fact that the invitation for his honoring in the skies has commenced without delay.

---

[8] *Shifā of Qāḍī `Iyāḍ: Chapter Regarding the Miracle of 'Isrā'*

[9] *Nasīm al-Riyāḍ: Volume 3, Chapter Regarding the Miracle of 'Isrā'*

## THE STORY OF MI`RĀJ IN THE NARRATION OF SAYYIDUNĀ 'ANAS BIN MĀLIK[10] رَضِيَ اللَّهُ عَنْهُ

The narration of Sayyidunā 'Anas bin Mālik رَضِيَ اللَّهُ عَنْهُ, the companion of Sayyidunā Rasūl Allāh صَلَّى اللَّهُ عَلَيْهِ وَسَلَّمَ, has been said to be the most superior narration in the subject of *'Isrā'* and *Mi`rāj* by 'Imām Qāḍī `Iyāḍ رَحِمَهُ ٱللَّهُ. *Nasīm al-Riyāḍ* mentions that this is due to the reason that it is the most detailed regarding this occurrence and the most authentic, as it has been included in the *Ṣaḥīḥ* of the renowned 'Imām Muslim رَحِمَهُ ٱللَّهُ.[11]

Some details of the journey not mentioned by Sayyidunā 'Anas رَضِيَ اللَّهُ عَنْهُ in this narration will also be mentioned in this section within its commentary. The narration states:

عن أنس بن مالك رضي الله عنه أن رسول الله صلى الله عليه وسلم قال أتيت بالبراق وهو دابة أبيض طويل فوق الحمار ودون البغل يضع حافره عند منتهى طرفه

*"It is narrated from 'Anas bin Mālik, may Allāh be pleased with him, that the Messenger of Allāh, may Allāh send blessing upon him and salutation, stated, 'I was brought the Burāq, which is a white animal, taller than the donkey and shorter than the mule whose hoof would reach to the extent of the gaze.'"*

---

[10] *As mentioned in the Shifā of Qāḍī `Iyāḍ: Chapter Regarding the Miracle of 'Isrā'*

[11] *Nasīm al-Riyāḍ: Volume 3, Chapter Regarding the Miracle of 'Isrā'*

## THE BURĀQ

In this part of the narration, Sayyidunā Rasūl Allāh ﷺ describes the mode of his transportation on the night of *Mi`rāj*. He explains that this creature that was brought to him on this night was named "*Burāq*." This was a creature from amongst the animals in *Jannah*. The name of this creature either originates from the root of *barīq*, which denotes glow, due to the immense glow of the creature, or from the word *barq*, which means thunder, due to the lightning-speed of the animal.[12] It was the rapid speed at which the animal traveled due to which the Messenger of Allāh ﷺ described that its hoof would reach the extent of the gaze; as far as the vision travels is equal to one step of this creature.

Citing 'Ibn al-Munīr, *Nasīm al-Riyāḍ* mentions that the *Burāq* was only brought to the Messenger of Allāh ﷺ on this night as a form of expressing love and bestowing honor. Had Allāh سُبْحَانَهُ وَتَعَالَىٰ willed, He could have allowed His Messenger ﷺ to travel wherever He wished without the means of such transportation, but He sent the means of transportation as a form of welcoming for the Beloved Messenger ﷺ. It is the custom of kings to make travel arrangements when their beloved is summoned. Allāh سُبْحَانَهُ وَتَعَالَىٰ is the Lord of All Kings, and He is summoning the one who is most beloved to Him ﷺ.

---

[12] *ibid*

The narration further states:

قال فركبته حتى أتيت بيت المقدس فربطته بالحلقة التي يربط بها الأنبياء

ثم دخلت المسجد فصليت فيه ركعتين

*"He said, 'So I rode it until I reached Bayt al-Maqdis. Thereupon, I tied it to the ring which the prophets tie it to, then I entered the Masjid and prayed two rak`ah in it.'"*

## TYING THE BURĀQ

Sayyidunā Rasūl Allāh ﷺ mentions here that he rode the *Burāq* until he reached *Masjid 'Aqṣā* and he tied the *Burāq* to a ring which other prophets عَلَيْهِمُ ٱلسَّلَامُ also tie it on.

*Nasīm al-Riyāḍ* mentions that this may be an indication that other prophets عَلَيْهِمُ ٱلسَّلَامُ had also rode the *Burāq* and this was the same ring they would tie the *Burāq* to.[13]

## THE PRAYER

Sayyidunā Rasūl Allāh ﷺ, upon entering the Masjid, prayed two *rak`ah*. However, this was a time in which the five *ṣalāh* had not yet been made an obligation on Sayyidunā Rasūl Allāh ﷺ and his nation. Thus, there is a difference of opinion regarding which *ṣalāh* was prayed in this instance. One position says that the *ṣalāh* prayed here was *Taḥīyah al-Masjid*,

---

[13] *ibid*

the prayer one is to pray as an expression of reverence to the Masjid upon entering.

It is also said, however, that one *ṣalāh* had been made obligatory at this point in time, but there is a difference regarding which time that *ṣalāh* was prayed. It was after this that the five *ṣalāh* were made obligatory and in the beginning, the timings of these prayers were not specified. Thus, the Muslims would pray whenever they wished; they could pray either as a congregation or scattered. Eventually, the timings of the five *ṣalāh* were specified.[14]

Further detail of the prayer performed on this night in *Bayt al-Maqdis* is found in various other narrations. These narrations show that the prayer performed on this night was not an ordinary prayer; it was one in which Allāh's most beloved, Sayyidunā Muḥammad Rasūl Allāh ﷺ led the other prophets عَلَيْهِمُ السَّلَامُ in prayer, proving his superiority amongst the most superior.

In one narration[15] from Sayyidunā 'Anas رَضِيَ اللَّهُ عَنْهُ, he states:

أنه صلى الله عليه وسلم صلى بالأنبياء ببيت المقدس

*"That he, may Allāh send blessing upon him and salutation, prayed with the prophets in Bayt al-Maqdis."*

This narration shows that the prayer performed was with the prophets of Allāh عَلَيْهِمُ السَّلَامُ, but several other narrations prove who it was to lead them in prayer.

---

[14] *ibid*

[15] *Shifā of Qāḍī `Iyāḍ: Chapter Regarding the Miracle of 'Isrā'*

The narration[16] of Sayyidunā 'Abū Hurayrah رَضِيَ ٱللَّهُ عَنْهُ states that the Messenger of Allāh said:

وقد رأيتني في جماعة من الأنبياء فحانت الصلاة فأممتهم

*"I had seen myself in a congregation of the prophets. Then, as ṣalāh time came, I led them all."*

This position of leading all the prophets عَلَيْهِمُ ٱلسَّلَامُ in *ṣalāh* was not a position he took on by his own will; this was the will of Allāh سُبْحَانَهُ وَتَعَالَىٰ. A narration[17] of Sayyidunā `Alī al-Murtaḍā رَضِيَ ٱللَّهُ عَنْهُ states:

ثم أخذ الملك بيد محمد صلى الله عليه وسلم فقدمه فأم أهل السماء فيهم آدم ونوح

*"Then the angel took the hand of Muḥammad, may Allāh send blessing upon him and salutation, then took him ahead. Then, he led the ones of the sky. Amongst them were 'Ādam and Nūḥ."*

This is the virtue and stature granted to the Most Beloved of Allāh صَلَّى ٱللَّهُ عَلَيْهِ وَسَلَّمَ. This congregation includes the most superior creations of Allāh سُبْحَانَهُ وَتَعَالَىٰ, yet in this manner, Allāh سُبْحَانَهُ وَتَعَالَىٰ clarifies to all that the one who is even superior to them is His Beloved صَلَّى ٱللَّهُ عَلَيْهِ وَسَلَّمَ.

---

16 *ibid*

17 *ibid*

The narration of Sayyidunā 'Anas bin Mālik رَضِيَ اللَّهُ عَنْهُ continues to say:

ثم خرجت فجاءني جبريل بإناء من خمر وإناء من لبن فاخترت اللبن

فقال جبريل اخترت الفطرة

*"Then I exited and Jibrīl approached me with a vessel of wine and a vessel of milk, so I chose the milk. So Jibrīl said, 'You have selected disposition.'"*

## THE OPTIONS

In this portion of the narration, it is seen that the Messenger of Allāh صَلَّى اللَّهُ عَلَيْهِ وَسَلَّمَ is offered two options: wine and milk. These options denoted various states of mankind, and the selection of Sayyidunā Rasūl Allāh صَلَّى اللَّهُ عَلَيْهِ وَسَلَّمَ would determine the state of his nation.

One option that is seen in this narration is that of wine. This wine was a symbol to all greed for evil and lust. Had the Beloved of Allāh صَلَّى اللَّهُ عَلَيْهِ وَسَلَّمَ selected the wine, the state of his followers would be altered as such.

In various other narrations of this occurrence, two more options are found: honey and water.

The option of honey is said to have depicted the splendor of the worldly life including its bliss and sweetness. The selection of honey would have led the nation to find delight in the temporary life of the world and would thus be a means for them becoming negligent of the hereafter.

The option of water symbolized drowning. The selection of water would lead to the nation drowning themselves in the gathering of wealth and riches becoming unconcerned of their responsibilities as slaves of Allāh سُبْحَانَهُ وَتَعَالَى.[18]

## THE SELECTION

Upon the selection of milk made by Sayyidunā Rasūl Allāh صَلَّى ٱللَّٰهُ عَلَيْهِ وَسَلَّمَ, Sayyidunā Jibrīl عَلَيْهِ ٱلسَّلَامُ states that, by his selection, Sayyidunā Rasūl Allāh صَلَّى ٱللَّٰهُ عَلَيْهِ وَسَلَّمَ has chosen disposition. The Arabic word used here to describe disposition was *fiṭrah*. This word has a meaning much deeper than just disposition. This disposition is in reference to human nature, that which Allāh سُبْحَانَهُ وَتَعَالَى has created man upon: 'Islām and steadfastness.

Amongst the two choices, milk was the one to denote human nature as this is something which is not only a delectable drink, but also a healthy form of nourishment for man, and its qualities allow for satisfaction to be achieved quickly. This is the reason for which it is the primary source of nourishment in children.[19]

---

[18] *Sharḥ al-Shifā, Mullā `Alī al-Qārī: Volume 1, Chapter Regarding the Miracle of 'Isrā'*

[19] *Nasīm al-Riyāḍ: Volume 3, Chapter Regarding the Miracle of 'Isrā'*

The narration then begins to describe the journey to the skies:

ثم عرج بنا إلى السماء فاستفتح جبريل فقيل من أنت قال جبريل قيل ومن معك قال محمد قيل وقد بعث إليه قال قد بعث إليه ففتح لنا فإذا أنا بآدم صلى الله عليه وسلم فرحب بي ودعا لي بخير

*"Then he raised us up to the sky and Jibrīl requested for it to be opened. It was said, 'Who are you?' He said, 'Jibrīl.' It was said, 'Who is with you?' He said, 'Muḥammad.' It was said, 'Has he been sent for?' He said, 'He has been sent for.' So, he opened for us. Then, there I was with 'Ādam, may Allāh send blessing upon him and salutation, so he welcomed me and wished me well."*

In this portion of the narration, the journey to the skies commences and the lofty rank of Allāh's beloved ﷺ is made even more manifest by the wondrous nature of this journey.

## HE RAISED US UP TO THE SKY

While describing the ascent into the skies, Sayyidunā Rasūl Allāh ﷺ states, "He raised us up to the sky." The pronoun "he" is referring to Sayyidunā Jibrīl عَلَيْهِ السَّلَام and the word "us" refers to himself and the *Burāq*.

## SEEKING PERMISSION

As they approach the first sky, Sayyidunā Jibrīl عَلَيْهِ ٱلسَّلَام seeks permission for entering either vocally or by knocking. The apparent position is that he sought permission by knocking, as his voice would be recognized by the angels who were appointed as doorkeepers.[20]

It is seen in this narration that Sayyidunā Jibrīl عَلَيْهِ ٱلسَّلَام seeks permission to enter, whereas his rank and stature amongst the angels suggests that he has no need for such permission. Sayyidunā Jibrīl عَلَيْهِ ٱلسَّلَام is the head of the angels and of the highest rank, and so the inevitable question arises: why did he seek permission to enter?

'Imām Khifājī رَحِمَهُ ٱللَّٰه cites 'Ibn al-Munīr in this matter as he mentions that on this night, the gates of the skies were locked and were to only be opened for the master of the skies, Rasūl Allāh صَلَّى ٱللَّٰهُ عَلَيْهِ وَسَلَّم.[21] This was another one of the many ways by which Allāh سُبْحَانَهُ وَتَعَالَىٰ bestowed honor unto His Beloved on this night.

Mullā `Alī al-Qārī رَحِمَهُ ٱللَّٰه mentions that the reason Sayyidunā Jibrīl عَلَيْهِ ٱلسَّلَام was further questioned even after the angels learned it was him at the door was that this was not the usual habit of Sayyidunā Jibrīl عَلَيْهِ ٱلسَّلَام. The fact that he sought the

---

[20] *ibid*

[21] *ibid*

opening of the gate informed them that there was someone who accompanied him.[22]

After the journey to the first sky, the Noble Messenger ﷺ makes mention of the journey beyond:

ثم عرج بنا إلى السماء الثانية فاستفتح جبرئيل فقيل من أنت قال جبرئيل قيل ومن معك قال محمد قيل وقد بعث إليه قال قد بعث إليه ففتح لنا فإذا أنا بابني الخالة عيسى ابن مريم ويحي بن زكريا صلى الله عليهما فرحبا بي ودعوا لي بخير

*"Then he took us to the second sky and Jibra'īl requested opening. It was said, 'Who are you?' He said, 'Jibra'īl.' It was said, 'Who is with you?' He said, 'Muḥammad.' It was said, 'Has he been sent for?' He said, 'He has been sent for.' So, he opened for us and there I was with the maternal cousins, `Īsā, the son of Maryam, and Yaḥyā, the son of Zakarīyā, may Allāh send blessings on them both. They welcomed me and wished me well."*

---

[22] *Sharḥ al-Shifā, Mullā `Alī al-Qārī: Volume 1, Chapter Regarding the Miracle of 'Isrā'*

## REPETITION OF QUESTIONS

In this portion of the narration, it is seen that the angels appointed for gatekeeping at the second sky asked Sayyidunā Jibrīl عَلَيْهِ ٱلسَّلَام the same questions before admitting his entrance. One reason for this could be the fact that those of one sky are unaware of the occurrences in other skies. Another reason could be that the angels were gratifying their senses by this conversation.[23] Hearing of the arrival of their master, Sayyidunā Rasūl Allāh صَلَّى ٱللَّٰهُ عَلَيْهِ وَسَلَّمَ, was of immense pleasure to them and were thus having Sayyidunā Jibrīl عَلَيْهِ ٱلسَّلَام repeat this time and time again to increase their pleasure.

After this journey to the second sky, the Messenger of Allāh صَلَّى ٱللَّٰهُ عَلَيْهِ وَسَلَّمَ continues his ascension:

ثم عرج بنا إلى السماء الثالثة فذكر مثل الأول ففتح لنا فإذا أنا بيوسف صلى الله عليه وسلم وإذا هو قد أعطي شطر الحسن فرحب بي ودعا لي بخير

*"Then he took us to the third sky and the same as before was mentioned, so he opened for us and there I was with Yūsuf, may Allāh send blessings upon him and salutation, all while he had been granted a portion of beauty. He welcomed me and wished me well."*

---

[23] *ibid*

## A PORTION OF BEAUTY

Whilst describing Sayyidunā Yūsuf عَلَيْهِ ٱلسَّلَامُ, Sayyidunā Rasūl Allāh صَلَّى ٱللَّٰهُ عَلَيْهِ وَسَلَّمَ makes mention of the beauty he possessed. However, he mentions that this beauty that was granted to him was a portion of beauty. What his beauty was a portion of has been discussed, but the position in this regard which has rose to be the most apparent position is that the renowned beauty of Sayyidunā Yūsuf عَلَيْهِ ٱلسَّلَامُ was just a part of the unmatched beauty and attraction possessed by Allāh's most Beloved Messenger, Sayyidunā Muḥammad صَلَّى ٱللَّٰهُ عَلَيْهِ وَسَلَّمَ.[24] Receiving a portion from the beauty of Sayyidunā Rasūl Allāh صَلَّى ٱللَّٰهُ عَلَيْهِ وَسَلَّمَ allowed for Sayyidunā Yūsuf عَلَيْهِ ٱلسَّلَامُ to be known and remembered by the extraordinary beauty he possessed.

The narration goes on to say:

ثم عرج بنا إلى السماء الرابعة وذكر مثله فإذا أنا بإدريس فرحب بي ودعا لي بخير قال الله تعالى ورفعناه مكانا عليا

*"Then he took us up to the fourth sky and the same was mentioned, so there I was with 'Idrīs. He welcomed me and wished me well. Allāh, the Exalted, stated, 'We raised him to a lofty station.'"*

[24] *ibid*

## A LOFTY STATION

While Sayyidunā Rasūl Allāh صَلَّى ٱللَّٰهُ عَلَيْهِ وَسَلَّمَ mentions his meeting with Sayyidunā 'Idrīs عَلَيْهِ ٱلسَّلَامُ, he mentions, in his description, a verse of the Noble Qur'ān. In this verse,[25] Allāh سُبْحَانَهُ وَتَعَالَىٰ informs that He had raised Sayyidunā 'Idrīs عَلَيْهِ ٱلسَّلَامُ to a lofty station and there are various positions regarding what exactly this lofty position is.

This is either referring to the obvious lofty status that Sayyidunā 'Idrīs عَلَيْهِ ٱلسَّلَامُ received in the world itself, or it is the fact that he was raised up to the skies as is apparent in this narration.

The details of this incident are found in a narration of Sayyidunā Ka`b 'Aḥbār رَضِيَ ٱللَّٰهُ عَنْهُ and some others. This narration explains that Sayyidunā 'Idrīs عَلَيْهِ ٱلسَّلَامُ had commanded the Angel of Death عَلَيْهِ ٱلسَّلَامُ to give him a taste of death, and so the Angel fulfilled this command by removing his soul and returning it back to him right away.

After this, Sayyidunā 'Idrīs عَلَيْهِ ٱلسَّلَامُ demanded that he be shown the hellfire so that he can be increased in the fear of Allāh and was thus delivered his demand. Upon reaching, he commanded Mālik عَلَيْهِ ٱلسَّلَامُ, the guard of the hellfire, to open the door so that he can pass over it and so he did.

Following the visit of the hellfire, Sayyidunā 'Idrīs عَلَيْهِ ٱلسَّلَامُ commanded the Angel of Death عَلَيْهِ ٱلسَّلَامُ to now take him to *Jannah*. He was taken to *Jannah*, had the door opened, and entered. After some passing of time, the Angel of Death

---

[25] *Sūrah Maryam: 57*

requested that Sayyidunā 'Idrīs عَلَيْهِ ٱلسَّلَام return to his place to which he responded, "Allāh has stated that every soul shall taste death, and I have tasted it. He has also stated that everyone will pass over the hellfire, and I have passed over it. Now, I have reached *Jannah* and Allāh has stated that they (those who enter it) will not be taken out of it, so why do you ask me to leave?" At this time, Allāh سُبْحَانَهُ وَتَعَالَىٰ revealed to the Angel of Death عَلَيْهِ ٱلسَّلَام that all that Sayyidunā 'Idrīs عَلَيْهِ ٱلسَّلَام had done, including the entrance of *Jannah*, was by the permission of Allāh سُبْحَانَهُ وَتَعَالَىٰ and now, by the permission of Allāh سُبْحَانَهُ وَتَعَالَىٰ, he should be left to live in *Jannah*.[26]

After this meeting with Sayyidunā 'Idrīs عَلَيْهِ ٱلسَّلَام, the Messenger of Allāh صَلَّى ٱللَّهُ عَلَيْهِ وَسَلَّمَ continues to ascend to heights beyond, and mentions:

ثم عرج بنا إلى السماء الخامسة فذكر مثله فإذا أنا بهارون فرحب بي ودعا لي بخير ثم عرج بنا إلى السماء السادسة فذكر مثله فإذا أنا بموسى فرحب بي ودعا لي بخير ثم عرج بنا إلى السماء السابعة فذكر مثله فإذا أنا بإبراهيم مسندا ظهره إلى البيت المعمور وإذا هو يدخله كل يوم سبعون ألف ملك لا يعودون إليه

*"Then, he lifted us to the fifth sky and the same was mentioned, so there I was with Hārūn. He welcomed me and wished me well. He then raised us to the sixth sky and the same was mentioned, so there I was with Mūsā. He welcomed me and wished me well. Then, he raised us to the seventh sky, so there I was with 'Ibrāhīm as he leaned his back to Bayt Ma`mūr while every day 70,000 angels enter it and do not return to it."*

---

[26] *Details summarized from Khazā'in al-`Irfān: Sūrah Maryam: 57*

## BAYT MA`MŪR

*Bayt Ma`mūr* is a structure which the angels circumambulate and make *Ḥajj* to as a form of worship. This structure in the skies is parallel to the *Ka`bah* which is on land. The word "*ma`mūr*" denotes the meaning of a populous place and due to this structure being densely populated by angels, it is called *ma`mūr*. Another name for this blessed location is *al-Ḍurāḥ*.[27]

## LEANING ON BAYT MA`MŪR

As Sayyidunā Rasūl Allāh صَلَّىٱللَّٰهُعَلَيۡهِوَسَلَّمَ describes his meeting with Sayyidunā 'Ibrāhīm عَلَيۡهِٱلسَّلَامُ, he mentions that Sayyidunā 'Ibrāhīm عَلَيۡهِٱلسَّلَامُ was leaning on *Bayt Ma`mūr*. The question that arises here is that this place is one of much virtue and worthy of much reverence, so why is Sayyidunā 'Ibrāhīm عَلَيۡهِٱلسَّلَامُ leaning against such a place of blessings?

Though there is much discussion in this matter, one position that stands out over the rest is one that shows the undisputed superiority of Sayyidunā Rasūl Allāh صَلَّىٱللَّٰهُعَلَيۡهِوَسَلَّمَ over all of Allāh's creations. This position explains that the reason Sayyidunā 'Ibrāhīm عَلَيۡهِٱلسَّلَامُ was leaning on such a virtuous place was so that he can greet and face the Master of All Virtue and the Beloved of Allāh صَلَّىٱللَّٰهُعَلَيۡهِوَسَلَّمَ, in a manner he is deserving of.[28]

---

27 *Nasīm al-Riyāḍ: Volume 3, Chapter Regarding the Miracle of 'Isrā'*

28 *ibid*

## MEETING THE PROPHETS

Up to this point in the narration, it is seen that Sayyidunā Rasūl Allāh ﷺ met several prophets including Sayyidunā 'Ibrāhīm عَلَيْهِ ٱلسَّلَامُ at the last sky. The question, however, is why these prophets in particular? Is there any significance in meeting these particular prophets of the 124,000, more or less?

Is the reason that the prophets honored by the meeting of Sayyidunā Rasūl Allāh ﷺ in the skies received this honor due to them being the *'ūlū al-`azm* messengers, those who are the most superior of them?

If this is the case, then why did Sayyidunā Hārūn عَلَيْهِ ٱلسَّلَامُ, for example, receive this honor and not Sayyidunā Nūḥ عَلَيْهِ ٱلسَّلَامُ, while he is amongst the list of the *'ūlū al-`azm* and not Sayyidunā Hārūn عَلَيْهِ ٱلسَّلَامُ or Sayyidunā 'Ādam عَلَيْهِ ٱلسَّلَامُ?

Upon this, it is said that there is a wisdom behind the meeting of each particular prophet in the skies. The sight of each of these prophets was an insight to the future occurrences in the blessed life of Sayyidunā Rasūl Allāh ﷺ.

On the first sky, the Beloved Messenger of Allāh ﷺ met Sayyidunā 'Ādam عَلَيْهِ ٱلسَّلَامُ. In the life of Sayyidunā 'Ādam عَلَيْهِ ٱلسَّلَامُ, it is seen that Sayyidunā 'Ādam عَلَيْهِ ٱلسَّلَامُ left paradise and came to the Earth, and this rooted from his enmity with the *shayṭān*. Seeing Sayyidunā 'Ādam عَلَيْهِ ٱلسَّلَامُ was a hint to the fact that Sayyidunā Rasūl Allāh ﷺ would also migrate from one place to another, and this was seen as he migrated from the city of *Makkah Mukarramah* to the city of *Madīnah Munawwarah* due to the grief caused to him by the people.

The sight of Sayyidunā Yaḥyā عَلَيْهِ السَّلَام and Sayyidunā `Īsā عَلَيْهِ السَّلَام was an indication to the animosity of the Jews that would be faced by Sayyidunā Rasūl Allāh صَلَّى ٱللَّٰهُ عَلَيْهِ وَسَلَّمَ. This nation was the one that martyred Sayyidunā Yaḥyā عَلَيْهِ السَّلَام and attempted to martyr Sayyidunā `Īsā عَلَيْهِ السَّلَام. They would be the ones who attempted to do the same to Sayyidunā Rasūl Allāh صَلَّى ٱللَّٰهُ عَلَيْهِ وَسَلَّمَ.

Seeing Sayyidunā Yūsuf عَلَيْهِ السَّلَام was a hint at the fact that just as the wrongs done to Sayyidunā Yūsuf عَلَيْهِ السَّلَام became a means of his latter success and majesty, Sayyidunā Rasūl Allāh صَلَّى ٱللَّٰهُ عَلَيْهِ وَسَلَّمَ would find the same. Furthermore, when Sayyidunā Yūsuf عَلَيْهِ السَّلَام ascended to this position, he forgave those who had wronged him, and such was done by Sayyidunā Rasūl Allāh صَلَّى ٱللَّٰهُ عَلَيْهِ وَسَلَّمَ upon the conquest of *Makkah Mukarramah.*

The vision of Sayyidunā Hārūn عَلَيْهِ السَّلَام was indicative of the hate that he once received from his nation turning into love, such that his people began giving him preference over his more superior brother, Sayyidunā Mūsā عَلَيْهِ السَّلَام. This, too, can be witnessed in the blessed life of Sayyidunā al-Muṣṭafā صَلَّى ٱللَّٰهُ عَلَيْهِ وَسَلَّمَ as the people who once despised him fell uncontrollably into his love.

Seeing Sayyidunā 'Idrīs عَلَيْهِ السَّلَام shows much wisdom as well. Sayydiunā 'Idrīs عَلَيْهِ السَّلَام was the first to write by pen, despite his lofty rank and stature. In his day, writing was seen as a job for those employed for it specifically; it was a job for those of low status.

Despite this, Sayyidunā 'Idrīs عَلَيْهِ السَّلَام showed the virtue of the pen and wrote with it, proving that this was not just for those of low stature. This foreshadowed the fact that Sayyidunā Rasūl Allāh صَلَّى ٱللَّٰهُ عَلَيْهِ وَسَلَّمَ would have written letters sent across the horizons spreading the message of 'Islām.

The meeting of Sayyidunā Musā عَلَيْهِ ٱلسَّلَامُ foreshadowed Sayyidunā Rasūl Allāh's صَلَّى ٱللَّٰهُ عَلَيْهِ وَسَلَّمَ conquest of *Makkah Mukarramah* and the subduing of those who once mocked his message. This is what was seen in the life of Sayyidunā Mūsā عَلَيْهِ ٱلسَّلَامُ as he defeated Fir`awn and subdued those who once mocked him.

Seeing Sayyidunā 'Ibrāhīm عَلَيْهِ ٱلسَّلَامُ on the final sky whilst leaning on *Bayt Ma`mūr* was indicative of Sayyidunā Rasūl Allāh's صَلَّى ٱللَّٰهُ عَلَيْهِ وَسَلَّمَ state towards the end of his apparent life in his *Ḥajj*.[29]

The narration continues the description of this blessed journey:

ثم ذهب بي إلى سدرة المنتهى وإذا ورقها كآذان الفيلة وإذا ثمرها كالقلال قال فلما غشيها من أمر الله ما غشى تعيرت فما أحد من خلق الله يستطيع أن ينعتها من حسنها

*"Then, he took me to Sidrah al-Muntahā as its leaves were like the ears of elephants and its fruits were like clay pots. He said, 'So, when what covers enveloped it due to the command of Allāh, it changed so that none from the creation of Allāh would be able to describe it because of its beauty.'"*

[29] *ibid*

## THE SIDRAH AL-MUNTAHĀ

In this part of the narration, the Beloved of Allāh ﷺ approaches the *Sidrah al-Muntahā*. This station is said to be the place where the knowledge of creation ceases.[30] This can also be seen in the name of this blessed tree as well, as the word "*muntahā*" denotes the extent or limit of something.

Of the many wondrous qualities of this blessed tree, one is the fact that it resembles perfection of faith, that which is made up of three: utterance, intention, and action.

The widespread shadows cast by this magnificent tree represents the action that is a result of faith and extends throughout the lives of the believers.

The taste found within the fruits of this tree depict intention. Taste is a quality that cannot be determined unless the onlooker bites into the fruit, and such is this aspect of faith. Intention is only apparent to the beholder. Its pleasance will only be found once it is adapted for one's own self.

The fragrance that the *Sidrah al-Muntahā* emits represents statements which stem from faith. Scent is a quality which can be determined from afar and without direct involvement. In this manner, the beauty within the word spoken by the true believer can be sensed from afar. One does not require faith to witness the beauty of faith which is expressed by the way the believers speak.[31]

---

[30] *Sharḥ al-Shifā, Mullā `Alī al-Qārī: Volume 1, Chapter Regarding the Miracle of 'Isrā'*

[31] *ibid*

The narration goes on to say:

فأوحى الله إلي ما أوحى ففرض علي خمسين صلاة في كل يوم وليل

*"So Allāh revealed to me whatever He revealed, and thus mandated upon me 50 ṣalāh in every day and night."*

## THE REVELATION

This statement of Allāh's Messenger ﷺ is in accordance with the description of the revelations of this night as mentioned in the Qur'ān. Allāh سُبْحَانَهُ وَتَعَالَىٰ states:

فَأَوْحَىٰٓ إِلَىٰ عَبْدِهِۦ مَآ أَوْحَىٰ

*"Now, He revealed to His servant whatever He revealed."* [32]

In this statement of Allāh's Messenger ﷺ describing the revelations of Allāh unto him on this night, there is much ambiguity. The unclarity left in this statement hints at the magnificence of these revelations and the fact that there was no need to reveal these things to others, as the intellect of man would not be able to comprehend those revelations.[33]

There are several statements regarding what these revelations could have been:

32 *Sūrah al-Najm: 10*

33 *Nasīm al-Riyāḍ: Volume 3, Chapter Regarding the Miracle of 'Isrā'*

- One statement is that none besides Sayyidunā Rasūl Allāh ﷺ knows of these revelations and was thus left ambiguous in the narration.
- Another statement is that it was *Sūrah al-'Inshirāḥ* which was revealed.
- A third statement is that this revelation was the fact that paradise is forbidden to every prophet until Sayyidunā Rasūl Allāh ﷺ enters it and to every nation until his nation enters it.[34]

In various other narrations, there are details of some conversations that took place on this night.

In *Mirqāh al-Mafātīḥ*, `Allāmah Mullā `Alī al-Qārī رَحِمَهُ ٱللَّهُ mentions a statement of 'Ibn al-Malik in which he mentions that the words commencing the *tashahhud* or *al-taḥīyāt* were the words by which Sayyidunā Rasūl Allāh ﷺ praised Allāh سُبْحَانَهُ وَتَعَالَىٰ.

The Messenger of Allah ﷺ stated:

التحيات لله والصلوات والطيبات

*"All of eternity is for Allāh, all prayers and all pure things."*

To this, Allāh سُبْحَانَهُ وَتَعَالَىٰ responded:

السلام عليك أيها النبي ورحمة الله وبركاته

*"Salutation be upon you O Prophet, the mercy of Allāh and His blessings."*

[34] *ibid*

Upon receiving *salām* from Allāh سُبْحَانَهُ وَتَعَالَىٰ, the Noble Messenger صَلَّى ٱللَّٰهُ عَلَيْهِ وَسَلَّمَ includes his slaves and states:

السلام علينا وعلى عباد الله الصالحين

*"Salutation be upon us and upon the righteous slaves of Allāh."*

Upon witnessing this, Sayyidunā Jibrīl عَلَيْهِ ٱلسَّلَامُ states:

أشهد أن لا إله إلا الله وأشهد أن محمدا عبده ورسوله

*"I bear witness that there is none worthy of worship except Allāh, and I testify that Muḥammad is His servant and His Messenger."*

'Ibn al-Malik states that this story of the *Mi`rāj* is included in *ṣalāh* as it is the *mi`raj* of the believers.[35]

Amongst these intimate conversations between Allāh سُبْحَانَهُ وَتَعَالَىٰ and His Beloved صَلَّى ٱللَّٰهُ عَلَيْهِ وَسَلَّمَ, one narration stands out in manifesting the love Allāh سُبْحَانَهُ وَتَعَالَىٰ showered His Beloved with.

This narration[36] states:

فقال تبارك وتعالى له سل فقال إنك اتخذت إبراهيم خليلا وأعطيته ملكا عظيما وكلمت موسى تكليما وأعطيت داود ملكا عظيما وألنت له الحديد وسخرت له الجبال وأعطيت سليمان ملكا عظيما وسخرت له الجن والإنس والشياطين والرياح وأعطيته ملكا لا ينبغي لأحد من بعده وعلمت عيسى التوراة والإنجيل وجعلته يبرئ الأكمه والأبرص وأعذته وأمه من الشيطان الرجيم فلم يكن له عليهما سبيل

---

35 *Mirqāh al-Mafātīḥ Sharḥ Mishkāh al-Maṣābīḥ: Book of Ṣalāh, Chapter of Tashahhud, Ḥadīth: 909*

36 *Shifā of Qāḍī `Iyāḍ: Chapter Regarding the Miracle of 'Isrā'*

*"So, He, the Blessed and Exalted, said to him, 'Ask.' So, he said, 'Indeed, You have taken 'Ibrāhīm as a friend and granted him a grand kingdom. You have spoken to Mūsā substantially. You have granted Dāwūd a grand kingdom, softened iron for him, and subjected the mountain for him. You have granted Sulaymān a great kingdom and subjected the jinn, the human, the devils, and the winds for him. You have granted him a kingdom unsuitable for anyone after him. You taught `Īsā the Tawrāh and the 'Injīl. You made him cure birth-blindness and the leprosy. You protected him and his mother from the accursed shayṭān so that there is no way for him over them two.'"*

The Messenger of Allāh ﷺ lists the bounties bestowed unto the prophets عَلَيْهِمُ السَّلَامُ who preceded him as He invites the showers of love and mercy from Allāh سُبْحَانَهُ وَتَعَالَىٰ. Upon the Messenger ﷺ inviting the manifestation of His love, He responds:

فقال له ربه تعالى قد اتخذتك خليلا وحبيبا فهو مكتوب في التوراة محمد حبيب الرحمن وأرسلتك إلى الناس كافة وجعلت أمتك هم الأولون وهم الآخرون وجعلت أمتك لا تجوز لهم خطبة حتى يشهدوا أنك عبدي ورسولي وجعلتك أول النبيين خلقا وآخرهم بعثا وأعطيتك سبعا من المثاني ولم أعطها نبيا قبلك وأعطيتك خواتيم سورة البقرة من كنز تحت عرشي لم أعطها نبيا قبلك وجعلتك فاتحا وخاتما

*"So, his Lord, the Exalted, said to him, 'I have taken you as a friend and beloved. Thus, it is inscribed in the Tawrāh, 'Muḥammad is the beloved of the Most Compassionate.' I have sent you to the people inclusive [of all]. I have made your nation those who are the first and last. I have made your nation for whom an address is not permissible until they testify that you are My servant and messenger. I have made you the first of*

*prophets in creation and the last of them in sending. I have granted you seven of the praises and I did not grant them to any prophet before you. I granted you the conclusions of Sūrah al-Baqarah from the treasure beneath My throne which I had not granted to any prophet before you. I have made you the opener and the seal.'"*

The love Allāh سُبۡحَانَهُۥ وَتَعَالَىٰ manifests to His Beloved صَلَّى ٱللَّهُ عَلَيۡهِ وَسَلَّمَ here is incredible and it is seen here that whatever bounties and blessings have been granted to the previous messengers of Allāh عَلَيۡهِمُ ٱلسَّلَامُ, the Master of Them All صَلَّى ٱللَّهُ عَلَيۡهِ وَسَلَّمَ has been granted those bounties in many folds and more.

As the narration of Sayyidunā 'Anas bin Mālik رَضِيَ ٱللَّهُ عَنۡهُ goes further into the journey, Sayyidunā Rasūl Allāh صَلَّى ٱللَّهُ عَلَيۡهِ وَسَلَّمَ states:

فنزلت إلى موسى فقال ما فرض ربك على أمتك قلت خمسين صلاة قال ارجع إلى ربك فاسأله التخفيف فإن أمتك لا يطيقون ذلك فإني قد بلوت بني إسرائيل وخبرتهم

*"Then, I descended to Mūsā, so he said, 'What has your Lord made an obligation upon your nation?' I said, '50 prayers.' He said, 'Return to your Lord, so ask Him for ease because your nation would not endure that. For indeed, I have tested Banū 'Isrā'īl and examined them.'"*

## WHY SAYYIDUNĀ MŪSĀ عَلَيۡهِ ٱلسَّلَامُ?

When Allāh سُبۡحَانَهُۥ وَتَعَالَىٰ ordained for the nation of Sayyidunā Rasūl Allāh صَلَّى ٱللَّهُ عَلَيۡهِ وَسَلَّمَ to pray *ṣalāh* 50 times in a day, Sayyidunā Mūsā عَلَيۡهِ ٱلسَّلَامُ was found awaiting him to hear this news.

Why is it that it was Sayyidunā Mūsā عَلَيْهِ السَّلَام who was concerned with the prayers ordained upon the nation of Sayyidunā Rasūl Allāh صَلَّى اللّٰهُ عَلَيْهِ وَسَلَّم? Why is it that he was the one to give his view in the matter when Sayyidunā Rasūl Allāh صَلَّى اللّٰهُ عَلَيْهِ وَسَلَّم would have to pass by Sayyidunā 'Ibrāhīm عَلَيْهِ السَّلَام on the seventh sky to get to Sayyidunā Mūsā عَلَيْهِ السَّلَام who was on the sixth sky?

The fact that it was Sayyidunā Mūsā عَلَيْهِ السَّلَام to express his view in this matter is due to the reason that Sayyidunā Mūsā's عَلَيْهِ السَّلَام nation had been given the obligation of *ṣalāh* before and he had a profound love for the nation of Sayyidunā Rasūl Allāh صَلَّى اللّٰهُ عَلَيْهِ وَسَلَّم.

When Sayyidunā Mūsā عَلَيْهِ السَّلَام had seen the virtues bestowed unto the nation of Sayyidunā Rasūl Allāh صَلَّى اللّٰهُ عَلَيْهِ وَسَلَّم in the Tawrāh, he asked Allāh سُبْحَانَهُ وَتَعَالَى to place him in that blessed nation. The concern Sayyidunā Mūsā عَلَيْهِ السَّلَام had was a result of this love and he feared that this nation would fall into hardship due to such burdensome obligations.[37]

## THE ENDURANCE OF THE NATION

Sayyidunā Mūsā عَلَيْهِ السَّلَام requested that the Beloved of Allāh صَلَّى اللّٰهُ عَلَيْهِ وَسَلَّم ask for ease in this matter because the nation would be unable to endure this burden of 50 prayers in one day. He did not say that the Messenger of Allāh صَلَّى اللّٰهُ عَلَيْهِ وَسَلَّم would not be able to bear its burden, although the obligation was for him as

[37] *Nasīm al-Riyāḍ: Volume 3, Chapter Regarding the Miracle of 'Isrā'*

well. This was not only a manifestation of the utmost respect and reverence he expressed in the court of Sayyidunā Rasūl Allāh ﷺ, but it was also because he knew of the strength and power of Sayyidunā Rasūl Allāh ﷺ over worship, and that the performance of 50 *ṣalāh* a day was not a burden to the one who carries the burden of both worlds ﷺ. This is the same strength by which he would practice *ṣawm wiṣāl*. This is a continuous fast which spans over several days at a time without any opening of the fast, an action his nation cannot bear physically and cannot practice legally.

## THE TEST OF BANŪ 'ISRĀ'ĪL

Sayyidunā Mūsā عَلَيْهِ السَّلَام was more convinced of the fact that this would be an unendurable burden for the nation of Sayyidunā al-Muṣṭafā ﷺ because he had examined his own nation with such tasks.

What makes this more of a reason for concern for the beloved nation of Sayyidunā Rasūl Allāh ﷺ is that the nation of Sayyidunā Mūsā عَلَيْهِ السَّلَام was unable to bear such a burden even with much stronger physicalities and longer lives.[38] If the Banū 'Isrā'īl were unable to endure such a burden with so much more physical strength, then how would the nation of Sayyidunā Rasūl Allāh ﷺ take this obligation?

38 *ibid*

The Beloved of Allāh ﷺ continues describing this blessed journey:

قال فرجعت إلى ربي فقلت يا رب خفف عن أمتي فحط عني خمسا فرجعت إلى موسى فقلت حط عني خمسا قال إن أمتك لا يطيقون ذلك فارجع إلى ربك فاسأله التخفيف قال فلم أزل أرجع بين ربي تعالى وبين موسى حتى قال يا محمد إنهن خمس صلوات كل يوم وليل لكل صلاة عشر فتلك خمسون صلاة ومن هم بحسنة فلم يعملها كتبت له حسنة فإن عملها كتبت له عشرا ومن هم بسيئة فلم يعملها لم تكتب شيئا فإن عملها كتبت سيئة واحدة

*"He said, 'I returned to my Lord, so I said, 'Oh my Lord, alleviate from my nation.' He relieved five from me, so I returned to Mūsā and I said, 'He relieved five from me.' He said, 'Your nation cannot endure that, so return to your Lord and ask Him for ease.' So, I continuously went back and forth between my Lord, the Exalted, and Mūsā until He said, 'O Muḥammad, indeed they are five ṣalāwāt in every day and night. For every ṣalāh is 10 so that is 50 ṣalāh. Whoever intends any good then does not do it, it is written for him as one good deed. So, if he does do it, 10 are written for him. Whoever intends any evil then does not do it, nothing is written for him. If he does do it, one bad deed is written.'''*

## THE WAIT OF SAYYIDUNĀ MŪSĀ

Every time Sayyidunā Rasūl Allāh ﷺ returns from the court of Allāh سُبْحَانَهُ وَتَعَالَىٰ, Sayyidunā Mūsā عَلَيْهِ ٱلسَّلَامُ is seen awaiting his arrival. What was it that caused Sayyidunā Mūsā عَلَيْهِ ٱلسَّلَامُ to await his arrival every time?

'Imām Sirāj Bulqīnī has mentioned that the intention of Sayyidunā Mūsā عَلَيْهِ ٱلسَّلَامُ was actually to repetitively gaze at the

Noble Messenger of Allāh ﷺ after having seen Allāh سُبْحَانَهُ وَتَعَالَىٰ.[39] This distinct pleasure found within the vision of he who had seen Allāh سُبْحَانَهُ وَتَعَالَىٰ was not unfamiliar to Sayyidunā Mūsā عَلَيْهِ ٱلسَّلَامُ. Sayyidunā Mūsā عَلَيْهِ ٱلسَّلَامُ had once asked to see Allāh سُبْحَانَهُ وَتَعَالَىٰ but was not granted his wish and was instead shown one manifestation *(tajallī)* to which he fainted and lost consciousness.

Allāh سُبْحَانَهُ وَتَعَالَىٰ mentions this in the Qur'ān as He states:

وَلَمَّا جَآءَ مُوسَىٰ لِمِيقَاتِنَا وَكَلَّمَهُۥ رَبُّهُۥ قَالَ رَبِّ أَرِنِيٓ أَنظُرْ إِلَيْكَ قَالَ لَن تَرَىٰنِى وَلَـٰكِنِ ٱنظُرْ إِلَى ٱلْجَبَلِ فَإِنِ ٱسْتَقَرَّ مَكَانَهُۥ فَسَوْفَ تَرَىٰنِى فَلَمَّا تَجَلَّىٰ رَبُّهُۥ لِلْجَبَلِ جَعَلَهُۥ دَكًّا وَخَرَّ مُوسَىٰ صَعِقًا فَلَمَّآ أَفَاقَ قَالَ سُبْحَـٰنَكَ تُبْتُ إِلَيْكَ وَأَنَا۠ أَوَّلُ ٱلْمُؤْمِنِينَ

*"And when Mūsā arrived at our covenant and his Lord spoke to him, he said, 'My Lord, show me so I will look at You.' He said, 'You will surely not be able to see Me, but look towards the mountain, so if it holds its place, then you shall soon see Me. So, when his Lord flashed His Light to the mountain, He sent it to ruins and Mūsā fell unconscious. So, when he recovered, he said, 'Glory to You! I repent to You, and I am the first of believers.'"* [40]

Here, Sayyidunā Mūsā عَلَيْهِ ٱلسَّلَامُ is seen asking Allāh سُبْحَانَهُ وَتَعَالَىٰ for His divine vision whereas not one narration or *'āyah* of the Qur'ān is in sight wherein Sayyidunā Rasūl Allāh ﷺ requests to see Allāh سُبْحَانَهُ وَتَعَالَىٰ. Sayyidunā Mūsā عَلَيْهِ ٱلسَّلَامُ asks for this bounty, but is refused it, and this station remained reserved

---

[39] *ibid*

[40] *Sūrah al-'A'rāf: 143*

for the beloved of Allāh, the Chosen One صَلَّى ٱللَّٰهُ عَلَيْهِ وَسَلَّمَ.

However, after this incident, no one was able to look at Sayyidunā Mūsā عَلَيْهِ ٱلسَّلَام and some would even pass away due to the majesty reflecting on his glowing face.[41] It was due to this reason that Sayyidunā Mūsā عَلَيْهِ ٱلسَّلَام began covering his noble face from the eyes of the people.

When Sayyidunā Mūsā عَلَيْهِ ٱلسَّلَام began veiling his face, his wife, Sayyidah Ṣafūrā رَضِيَ ٱللَّٰهُ عَنْهَا, began feeling distant and expressed dissatisfaction that she had not been able to see her husband's face since he had conversed with Allāh سُبْحَانَهُ وَتَعَالَىٰ. At the expression of this grief, Sayyidunā Mūsā عَلَيْهِ ٱلسَّلَام unveiled his blessed face, and the light of his face captured the gaze of his wife like the beaming rays of the sun. Upon seeing such breath-taking beauty, she immediately covered her face with her hand and asked Sayyidunā Mūsā عَلَيْهِ ٱلسَّلَام to make *du`ā'* that she remains his wife even in paradise.[42]

A further-detailed narrative of this occurrence is mentioned by Sayyidunā Muḥaddith Kabīr `Allāmah Ḍiyā' al-Muṣṭafā, may Allāh protect him. In his mention of this narrative, he explains that those who would look into the eyes of Sayyidunā Mūsā عَلَيْهِ ٱلسَّلَام would lose their eyesight. Thus, Sayyidunā Mūsā عَلَيْهِ ٱلسَّلَام would either veil his face or would lower his gaze in public.

The wife of Sayyidunā Mūsā عَلَيْهِ ٱلسَّلَام insistingly requested to look into his eyes despite being warned that not everyone bears the ability to do so.

Sayyidunā Mūsā عَلَيْهِ ٱلسَّلَام gave her permission as they agreed

---

[41] *Tafsīr al-Durr al-Manthūr, Sūrah al-'A`rāf: 143*

[42] *Tafsīr Rūḥ al-Bayān, Sūrah al-'A`rāf: 145*

that she would only look with one eye. She covered one eye with her hand and looked into his eyes with the other. She looked as long as she could bear until her eyesight was lost to the magnificence within his eyes. But this taste of the pleasure in seeing his eyes only grew due to this. So, she covered the damaged eye and sacrificed her other and only functioning eye to reap the pleasure within his sight.

It was the mercy of Allāh سُبْحَانَهُ وَتَعَالَىٰ that caused the eyesight to return to her first eye as the second lost function, but she continued this as Allāh سُبْحَانَهُ وَتَعَالَىٰ kept blessing her with eyesight in the eye she would purposely sacrifice for this view.

This went on as she would look with one eye and lose eyesight in the other, then regain her sight by the grace of Allāh سُبْحَانَهُ وَتَعَالَىٰ in the eye she was not seeing from. Eventually, Allāh سُبْحَانَهُ وَتَعَالَىٰ returned her sight into both eyes, and she began seeing better than she ever had before.[43]

If this was the case in seeing Sayyidunā Mūsā عَلَيْهِ ٱلسَّلَامُ, who had only seen one manifestation, one cannot even begin to imagine the pleasure in gazing at the one who has seen Allāh سُبْحَانَهُ وَتَعَالَىٰ, the noble and most superior messenger, Sayyidunā Muḥammad Rasūl Allāh صَلَّى ٱللَّٰهُ عَلَيْهِ وَسَلَّمَ.

It was this information that Sayyidunā Mūsā عَلَيْهِ ٱلسَّلَامُ had which caused him to wait for Sayyidunā Rasūl Allāh صَلَّى ٱللَّٰهُ عَلَيْهِ وَسَلَّمَ when he would return from seeing Allāh سُبْحَانَهُ وَتَعَالَىٰ. This was the pleasure Sayyidunā Mūsā عَلَيْهِ ٱلسَّلَامُ was in hopes of attaining by seeing Sayyidunā Rasūl Allāh صَلَّى ٱللَّٰهُ عَلَيْهِ وَسَلَّمَ.

---

43 *Mi`rāj Sharīf, Eik Mu`jizah*

Furthermore, in a narration mentioned in both *Ṣaḥīḥ al-Bukhārī* and *Ṣaḥīḥ Muslim*, the Messenger of Allāh ﷺ states:

من رآني فقد رأى الحق

*"Whoever has seen me has seen the truth."* [44]

Though the majority mentions that this narration entails that if someone has seen the Messenger of Allāh ﷺ in a dream, it was actually him that the person saw, there is another view regarding its meaning.

This position says that the meaning of this narration is that the one who sees Sayyidunā Rasūl Allāh ﷺ, it is as if he has seen *al-Ḥaqq*, Allāh سُبْحَانَهُ وَتَعَالَى. This is due to Sayyidunā Rasūl Allāh ﷺ being the greatest reflection of Allāh's سُبْحَانَهُ وَتَعَالَى majesty. It is just like saying one has conversed with Allāh سُبْحَانَهُ وَتَعَالَى when he has recited the Qur'ān.[45]

Furthermore, if one takes a deep dive into any of Allāh's سُبْحَانَهُ وَتَعَالَى superior creations, it will lead them to faith in a creator. For example, if one studies the human body and the manner in which all of its parts function together flawlessly, one will surely ponder the existence of a creator as such perfection cannot be mere coincidence. If one ponders upon the solar system and the perfection of the distance and relation of planets to one another, this too will lead a sincere individual to faith in a creator.

---

[44] *Mishkāh al-Maṣābīḥ: Book of Dreams*

[45] *Mir'ah al-Manājīḥ Sharḥ Mishkāh al-Maṣābīḥ: Book of Dreams (Muftī 'Aḥmad Yār Khān Na`īmī رَحِمَهُ ٱللَّٰهُ)*

Sayyidunā Rasūl Allāh ﷺ is the most superior creation of Allāh سُبْحَانَهُ وَتَعَالَىٰ and His greatest sign. Whereas studying and examining any of Allāh's سُبْحَانَهُ وَتَعَالَىٰ greatest signs and creations will lead one to faith in a creator, studying the depths of Sayyidunā Rasūl Allāh ﷺ leads to unshakable faith in Allāh's سُبْحَانَهُ وَتَعَالَىٰ existence.

Perhaps, this is what is meant by this meaning of the narration.

This may be one of the many possible reasons that Sayyidunā Mūsā عَلَيْهِ السَّلَامُ longed to view the Messenger of Allāh ﷺ time and time again.

The narration of Sayyidunā 'Anas bin Mālik is then concluded as Sayyidunā Rasūl Allāh ﷺ mentions:

قال فنزلت حتى انتهيت إلى موسى فأخبرته فقال ارجع إلى ربك فاسأله التخفيف فقال رسول الله صلى الله عليه وسلم فقلت قد رجعت إلى ربي حتى استحييت منه

*"He said, 'So, I descended until I stopped at Mūsā, then I informed him. He said, 'Return to your Lord, then ask Him for ease." So, the Messenger of Allāh, may Allāh send blessing upon him and salutation, said, 'I said I have returned to my Lord until I became shy of Him.'"*

## THE GIFT OF ṢALĀH

In this blessed journey of *Mi`rāj*, Allāh bestowed the gift of *ṣalāh* unto the believers. Despite *ṣalāh* being a gift, it is unfortunate that today many Muslims undermine the importance of *ṣalāh* and pay no heed to this obligation. It is the mercy of Allāh

سُبْحَانَهُ وَتَعَالَى that the nation is not burdened with 50 prayers in one day and thus, the believer should keep this in mind and responsibly offer his five prayers of the day.

A possible wisdom of bestowing this gift of *ṣalāh* unto the believers on the night of *'Isrā'* is that it is indicative of *ṣalāh* being a *mi`rāj*, or ascension, of the believers. By the means of *ṣalāh*, a believer ascends to his perfections and escalates in status. The *ṣalāh*, amongst the other forms of worship, is the one in which a slave presents himself in the court of Allāh سُبْحَانَهُ وَتَعَالَى and becomes engaged in intimate conversation with his Lord.[46]

This concludes the narration of Sayyidunā 'Anas bin Mālik رَضِيَ اللَّهُ عَنْهُ and the details of the blessed journey mentioned by him.

## THE EXTENT OF THE JOURNEY

In the narration of Sayyidunā 'Anas bin Mālik رَضِيَ اللَّهُ عَنْهُ, the journey in the skies was described up until the point of *Sidrah al-Muntahā*. However, several narrations and writings of scholars suggest that this journey continues past the *Sidrah al-Muntahā* up to the *Mustawā*, the *`Arsh*, and the spiritual journey goes even beyond.

46 *Sharḥ al-Shifā, Mullā `Alī al-Qārī: Volume 1, Chapter Regarding the Miracle of 'Isrā'*

## THE MUSTAWĀ

The narration of Sayyidunā 'Ibn `Abbās[47] رَضِيَ اللَّهُ عَنْهُمَا mentions:

ثم عرج بي حتى ظهرت بمستوى أسمع فيه صريف الأقلام

*"Then it raised me until I ascended Mustawā. I heard in it the movement of the pens."*

This station of *Mustawā* is after the *Sidrah al-Muntahā*, but the journey of Allāh's beloved صَلَّى اللَّهُ عَلَيْهِ وَسَلَّمَ continues even past this station.

## THE JOURNEY BEYOND

The 'Imām of the *'Ahl al-Sunnah*, Shaykh al-'Islām 'Imām 'Aḥmad Riḍā' رَحِمَهُ اللَّهُ, has written a pamphlet named *Munabbih al-Munyah li Wuṣūl al-Ḥabīb 'ilā al-`Arsh wa al-Ru'yah.*

In this compilation of two separate queries, one section details the various writings of the noble scholars in which they mention the continuation of the blessed journey not only past *Sidrah al-Muntahā*, but even past the *Mustawā* and the *`Arsh*.

A summary of one of these sections will be mentioned here and of the second section later on in this work.

---

[47] *Shifā of Qāḍī `Iyāḍ: Chapter Regarding the Miracle of 'Isrā'*

## THE PRINCIPLE

Firstly, the Noble 'Imām رَحِمَهُ ٱللَّٰهُ mentions that the writings of the noble scholars in this regard are all *ḥadīth*, albeit narrations graded *mursal*[48] or *mu`ḍal*[49] according to one categorization.

Such writings of the scholars are regarded as *ḥadīth*, especially when the narrators are credible and trusted, and the narration is regarding a matter in which there is nothing said based on personal judgment.

Furthermore, the *mursal* and *mu`ḍal* narrations are unanimously accepted in establishment of virtue. The fact that this matter has no room for personal judgment entails that it is being said due to existing proof.

Moreover, the affirmative narrations are given preference over the negative, as the absence of information does not entail information of absence.

Sayyidunā 'Imām 'Ibn al-Humām رَحِمَهُ ٱللَّٰهُ mentions the principle in this regard in *Fatḥ al-Qadīr:*

عدم النقل لا ينفي الوجود

*"The absence of narration does not negate occurrence."*

The Noble 'Imām mentions a statement from *Musallam al-Thubūt* defining a *mursal* narration:

---

48 *A mursal narration is one in which any tābi`ī says, "Rasūl Allāh* صَلَّىٱللَّٰهُعَلَيْهِوَسَلَّمَ *said..." (al-Tadhkirah)*

49 *A mu`ḍal narration is one in which two or more narrators are omitted (al-Tadhkirah)*

المرسل قول العدل قال رسول الله عليه الصلوة والسلام كذا

*"The mursal is the statement of an honest person that the Messenger of Allāh, upon him be blessing and salutation, said, 'so and so.'"*

This shows that if a credible and trusted individual attributes a statement to Allāh's messenger ﷺ, this attribution will be given consideration and is given regard.

Furthermore, a statement mentioned in *Fawātiḥ al-Raḥmūt* reads:

المرسل إن كان من صحابي يقبل مطلقا اتفاقا وإن كان من غيره فالأكثر ومنهم الإمام أبو حنيفة والإمام مالك والإمام أحمد رضي الله تعالى عنهم قالوا يقبل مطلقا إذا كان الراوي ثقة...

*"The mursal, if it is from a ṣaḥābī, it will be accepted unrestrictedly, unanimously. If it is from another, the majority, including 'Imām 'Abū Ḥanīfah, 'Imām Mālik, and 'Imām 'Aḥmad, may Allāh be pleased with them, say, 'It will be accepted unrestrictedly when the narrator is reliable…'"*

## *The Texts of the 'Imāms*

The renowned *Qaṣīdah Burdah* of 'Imām Būṣīrī رَحِمَهُ ٱللَّهُ states:

سريت من حرم ليلا إلى حرم

كما سرى البدر في داج من الظلم

*You traveled from a Ḥaram in the night to a Ḥaram*
*As the full moon travels in a dark night*

وبت ترقي إلى أن نلت منزلة

من قاب قوسين لم تدرك ولم ترم

*You excelled until you reached a station*
*Of two bows, which no one attained nor dared*

خفضت كل مقام بالإضافة إذ

نوديت بالرفع مثل المفرد العلم

*Every rank seems low in comparison to you since*
*You were invited [for Mi`rāj] to rise like a mighty flag*

فحزت كل فخار غير مشترك

وجزت كل مقام غير مزدحم

*You collected every unshared glory*
*And you passed through every station uncrowded*

This portion of the *Qaṣīdah Burdah* entails that the Noble Messenger ﷺ traveled throughout all of space. Moreover, the mention that these places were traveled uncrowded entails that from a part of the journey, the traveling was done alone.

Commenting on this, `Allāmah `Alī al-Qārī رَحِمَهُ ٱللَّٰهُ mentions that Sayyidunā Rasūl Allāh ﷺ exceeded the realm of space up until the station which is called *Qāba Qawsayn*, or the station of two bows and even beyond.

Furthermore, 'Imām 'Ibn Ḥajar Makkī رَحِمَهُ ٱللَّٰهُ states:

قال بعض الأئمة والمعاريج ليلة الإسراء عشرة سبعة في السٰموت والثامن إلى سدرة المنتهى والتاسع إلى المستوى والعاشر إلى العرش

*"Some of the 'Imāms said, 'The ascensions are 10 on the night of 'Isrā': seven are in the skies, the eighth is to Sidrah al-Muntahā, the ninth is to Mustawā, and the 10th is to the `Arsh.'"*

One narration mentioned by 'Imām Qasṭalānī رَحِمَهُ ٱللَّٰهُ and `Allāmah Zurqānī رَحِمَهُ ٱللَّٰهُ states:

قد ورد في الصحيح عن أنس رضي الله تعالى عنه قال لما عرج بي جبريل إلي سدرة المنتهٰي ودنا الجبار رب العزة فتدلى فكان قاب قوسين أو أدنى وتدليه على ما في حديث شريك كان فوق العرش

*"It has appeared in the Ṣaḥīḥ from 'Anas bin Mālik, may Allāh be pleased with him, that he said, 'When Jibrīl elevated me to Sidrah al-Muntahā and al-Jabbār, the Lord of Majesty, reeled me closer and closer, such that it was the length of two bows or less.' This growing closer according to what is in the narration of Sharīk was above the*

`Arsh."

Moreover, whereas some narrations denote that the Messenger of Allāh ﷺ surpassed the `Arsh, others claim that this was not the case.

This is seen in the statement of Shaykh Sulaymān رحمه الله in *Futūḥāt 'Aḥmadīyah*:

رقيه صلى الله تعالى عليه وسلم ليلة الإسراء من بيت المقدس إلى السّٰموت السبع إلى حيث شاء الله تعالى لكنه لم يجاوز العرش على الراجح

*"He, may Allāh send blessing upon him and salutation, was elevated on the night of 'Isrā' from Bayt al-Maqdis to the seven skies up to wherever Allāh, the Exalted, willed. However, he did not surpass the `Arsh, upon the preferred position."*

The Noble 'Imām 'Aḥmad Riḍā' رحمه الله concludingly mentions that there is no issue in the conflict of these narrations. This is because the journey of the physical body was up until the `Arsh as the `Arsh is the extent of space, and a body will not exist except in space. The journey beyond this was one of the heart.

However, this does not necessitate any deficiency in the journey as he physically traveled throughout all that was possible, and when space came to an end, he advanced by his pure soul.

*Note:* In these narrations, when the distance of two bows and growing closer is mentioned, this should not be interpreted as distance of location, as Allāh سبحانه وتعالى is free from the constraints of distance, location, and direction. This should be understood as a figurative closeness to the mercy of Allāh سُبْحَانَهُ وَتَعَالَىٰ which only Sayyidunā Rasūl Allāh صَلَّى ٱللَّٰهُ عَلَيْهِ وَسَلَّمَ attained.

This was a means for increasing his rank by allowing him to witness the secrets of the unseen.[50]

[50] *Shifā of Qāḍī `Iyāḍ: Chapter Regarding the Miracle of 'Isrā', Closeness*

CHAPTER THREE

# Beliefs Concerning the Mi`rāj

## THE IMPORTANCE OF BELIEF IN THE MI`RĀJ

### *Masjid Ḥarām to Bayt al-Maqdis*

The occurrence of the *Mi`rāj* is divided into three stages in terms of the degree of report confirming the portion of the journey.

The first stage of the journey commences at *Masjid Ḥarām* to *Bayt al-Maqdis*. The report confirming this portion of the journey is definitive as this is mentioned clearly in the Blessed Qur'ān.

The denier of this portion will be charged with unbelief.

## *From Land to the Skies*

The portion of the blessed journey wherein the Messenger of Allāh ﷺ ascended from the land and traveled throughout the skies is established by *ḥadīth mash-hūr*. This is a famous narration which is reported by a group of narrators.

Therefore, he who denies this portion of the blessed journey will not be charged with unbelief but will be labeled astray.

## *The Journey Beyond*

The journey from the skies to the heavens, the *`Arsh*, or beyond, is proven by *wāḥid* narrations. These are various narrations transmitted by solitary narrators.

The individual who denies the occurrence of this portion will not be deemed an unbeliever or astray but will be considered mistaken and to have committed an offense.[51]

## A DREAM OR A PHYSICAL JOURNEY?

Amongst the *'Ahl al-Sunnah*, there are two positions regarding the *Mi`rāj*. While some say that this was a journey which took place in a righteous dream shown to Sayyidunā Rasūl Allāh ﷺ, the dominant position is that this was a journey of his physical body.

---

[51] *al-Nibrās Sharḥ Sharḥ al-`Aqā'id al-Nasafīyah, Chapter: The Mi`rāj is True*

This difference, and the dominating position, is mentioned by Sayyidunā 'Imām al-Nawawī رَحِمَهُ ٱللَّهُ:[52]

فقيل إنما كان جميع ذلك في المنام والحق الذي عليه أكثر الناس ومعظم السلف وعامة المتأخرين من الفقهاء والمحدثين والمتكلمين أنه أسرى بجسده صلى الله عليه وسلم والآثار تدل عليه لمن طالعها وبحث عنها ولا يعدل عن ظاهرها إلا بدليل ولا إستحالة في حملها عليه فيحتاج إلى تأويل

*"So, it was said, 'Indeed, all of that was in a dream.' The truth is that which the majority of the people, the mass of the predecessors, the prevalence of the latter-coming of the fuqahā', muḥaddithūn, and theologists are upon: that he was granted 'Isrā' in his physical body, may Allāh send blessing upon him and salutation. The narrations indicate towards it for the one who studies them and investigates them. The apparent will not be abandoned except by evidence while there is no impossibility in applying it upon it (the apparent), such that it would require interpretation."*

This quote shows that not only does the dominant position denote that this journey was one of the physical body, but it shows that this is the position clearly expressed by the narrations. Those who adapt the position of the journey being a dream have diverged from the apparent meaning and have gone towards *ta'wīl*, or interpretation, of the literal meanings.

---

[52] *al-Minhāj Sharḥ Ṣaḥīḥ Muslim: The Chapter of 'Isrā' with Allāh's Messenger to the Skies and the Obligation of the Prayers*

However, there is only a requirement for *ta'wīl* in the case that other pieces of evidence oppose the literal meanings of the narration, or there is a legal barrier preventing the application on the apparent meaning. In this case, neither are found. Thus, there is no need for *ta'wīl*, and the literal meanings of the narrations will be adapted as the position.

## *The Evidence of the Opposition*

The school which regards the journey of *Mi`rāj* to be a dream presents various pieces of evidence in its case.

*First and Second Evidence*

Sayyidunā 'Amīr Mu`āwiyah رضي الله عنه was asked regarding the *Mi`rāj* and he responded:

كانت رؤيا صالحة

*"It was a righteous vision."*

Furthermore, the Noble Qur'ān states:

وَمَا جَعَلْنَا الرُّؤيَا الَّتِي أَرَيْنَاكَ إِلَّا فِتْنَةً لِّلنَّاسِ

*"And We did not make the vision which We showed you except a test for the people."* [53]

---

[53] *Sūrah al-'Isrā': 60*

*The Response*

Both aforementioned references of the opposition are seen using the word *ru'yā*, or vision, to describe this journey of *Mi`rāj*. However, after presenting these two pieces of evidence from the opposition, 'Imām Sa`d al-Dīn al-Taftāzānī رَحِمَهُ ٱللَّهُ responds by saying that this word *ru'yā* refers to the vision by eye.[54]

This entails that the journey was witnessed by the physical eye and was not a vision that was shown in sleep.

This is further confirmed by a statement of Sayyidunā 'Ibn `Abbās رَضِيَ ٱللَّهُ عَنْهُمَا:[55]

هي رؤيا عين رآها النبي صلى الله عليه وسلم لا رؤيا منام

*"It is a vision of the eye the Prophet, may Allāh send blessing upon him and salutation, saw. Not a vision of sleep."*

*Third Evidence*

The third form of support brought forth by the opposition is a narration of the mother of the believers, the beloved wife of Sayyidunā Rasūl Allāh صَلَّى ٱللَّهُ عَلَيْهِ وَسَلَّمَ, the honorable and virtuous, Sayyidatunā `Ā'ishah Ṣiddīqah رَضِيَ ٱللَّهُ عَنْهَا. The Mother of Believers رَضِيَ ٱللَّهُ عَنْهَا states:

---

[54] *Sharḥ al-`Aqā'id al-Nasafīyah, Chapter: The Mi`rāj is True*

[55] *The Shifā of Qāḍī `Iyāḍ: Chapter Regarding the Miracle of 'Isrā', The Reality of 'Isrā'*

ما فقد جسد محمد عليه السلام ليلة المعراج

*"The body of Muḥammad, upon him be salutation, was not away on the night of Mi`rāj."*

*The Response*

Sayyidunā 'Imām Sa`d al-Dīn al-Taftāzānī رَحِمَهُ ٱللَّهُ responds to those who use this narration in proving that the blessed journey was a dream by saying that the meaning of this is not that Sayyidunā Rasūl Allāh صَلَّى ٱللَّهُ عَلَيْهِ وَسَلَّمَ was not away from her. Rather, her saying that his blessed body was not away entails that the blessed body was not away from his blessed soul and that the journey was of the body and soul altogether.[56]

The Honorable `Allāmah `Abd al-`Azīz رَحِمَهُ ٱللَّهُ, author of *al-Nibrās*, further adds to this refutation by three points:[57]

I. The chain of transmission for this narration has been graded *ḍa`īf* or weak.
II. In the time of *Mi`rāj*, Sayyidatunā `Ā'ishah رَضِيَ ٱللَّهُ عَنْهَا was not yet married to Sayyidunā Rasūl Allāh صَلَّى ٱللَّهُ عَلَيْهِ وَسَلَّمَ, and nor was she at an age in which she possessed comprehension. According to some historians, she may not have even been born at this time. Thus, the narration of those present and aware at this time will be given preference over hers.

---

[56] *Sharḥ al-`Aqā'id al-Nasafīyah, Chapter: The Mi`rāj is True*

[57] *al-Nibrās Sharḥ Sharḥ al-`Aqā'id al-Nasafīyah, Chapter: The Mi`rāj is True*

III. The *Mi`rāj* has occurred twice. Once with the blessed body and once of the blessed soul on its own. This narration describes the second journey.

Moreover, it is known that this *Mi`rāj* commenced from the blessed city of *Makkah Mukarramah*, and the narrations have mentioned that Sayyidatunā `Ā'ishah رَضِيَ اللَّهُ عَنْهَا only moved in with the Messenger of Allāh صَلَّى اللَّهُ عَلَيْهِ وَسَلَّمَ in the blessed city of *Madīnah Munawwarah*.[58]

In any case, she was not in the company of Sayyidunā Rasūl Allāh صَلَّى اللَّهُ عَلَيْهِ وَسَلَّمَ at the time of this *Mi`rāj*.

## *A Cause of Disbelief*

Furthermore, it is known that the occurrence of this blessed journey became the reason for many leaving the folds of faith.[59] Upon hearing of such a miraculous and lengthy journey taking place in a short portion of the night, many were unable to submit their intellects to faith, and thus left the folds of 'Islām.

Had this journey been a dream, what was the barrier preventing belief in it?

Many people see lengthy dreams in their sleep which are felt to span over several days but awaken to realize that only some time has passed. Many see unbelievable and

---

58 *The Shifā of Qāḍī `Iyāḍ: Chapter Regarding the Miracle of 'Isrā', Refutation of the Proofs of Those Who Say it Was a Dream*

59 *Sharḥ al-`Aqā'id al-Nasafīyah, Chapter: The Mi`rāj is True*

unimaginable sights in their dreams, but no matter how absurd the dream may be, when one tells of the dream, there is no objection regarding whether the person has actually seen such a dream.

Had the journey of *Mi`rāj* been just a dream, there would be no case of people leaving the faith as there is no difficulty or challenge in believing in the occurrence of such a dream. The people would have accepted the claims with much ease.

The occurrences after the announcement of the *Mi`rāj* were contrary to this. Several disbelieved, and the enemies laughed and mocked such a claim.

It is narrated that the people rushed to Sayyidunā 'Abū Bakr رَضِيَ اللَّهُ عَنْهُ and said:

هل سمعت ما قال صاحبك

*"Have you heard what your master has said?"*

قال أنا أصدقه على أبعد من ذلك

*"He responded, 'I have verified him upon what is even more difficult to understand than that."*

It was from this day that Sayyidunā 'Abū Bakr رَضِيَ اللَّهُ عَنْهُ was given the title of *al-Ṣiddīq*, the very truthful one.[60] Sayyidunā 'Abū Bakr رَضِيَ اللَّهُ عَنْهُ showed the way of a believer and accepted the announcement of *Mi`rāj* with ease. He had not seen Allāh سُبْحَانَهُ وَتَعَالَى, the angels, heaven, or hell, and he believes in the existence of them all just by the trust in Sayyidunā Rasūl Allāh

[60] *al-Nibrās Sharḥ Sharḥ al-`Aqā'id al-Nasafiyah, Chapter: The Mi`rāj is True*

ﷺ, so what is the difficulty in believing in this blessed journey Allāh سُبْحَانَهُ وَتَعَالَىٰ had granted him?

Moreover, the verse of the Qur'ān brought forth by the opposition ascertains that this journey was not a dream as the *'āyah* refers to the vision as a test for the people,[61] and believing in the occurrence of a dream is not a test.

## SEEING ALLĀH سُبْحَانَهُ وَتَعَالَىٰ

The Noble and Beloved Messenger of Allāh ﷺ was bestowed countless bounties and forms of honoring in this blessed journey of *Mi`rāj*. Amongst these unfathomed treasures bestowed unto him is the honor of viewing Allāh سُبْحَانَهُ وَتَعَالَىٰ.

Though there is some difference in this regard, the fact that he, in fact, did see Allāh سُبْحَانَهُ وَتَعَالَىٰ on this night, is the dominant position and that of the majority.

In proof of this position, the first matter of discussion is whether it is even possible to see Allāh سُبْحَانَهُ وَتَعَالَىٰ.

The only valid position amongst the *'Ahl al-Sunnah* in this regard is that it is not only possible, but it will be bestowed unto the believers in paradise.

In proof of this, there is much evidence found in the Noble Qur'ān, the prophetic narrations, consensus, and the works of the pious predecessors.

---

61 *The Shifā of Qāḍī `Iyāḍ: Chapter Regarding the Miracle of 'Isrā': Refutation of the Proofs of Those Who Say it Was a Dream*

## *Evidence From the Glorious Qur'ān*

*First Evidence*

Allāh سُبْحَانَهُ وَتَعَالَىٰ states:

وُجُوهٌ يَوْمَئِذٍ نَّاضِرَةٌ

إِلَىٰ رَبِّهَا نَاظِرَةٌ

*"The faces on that day will be glowing.*
*To their Lord, looking."* [62]

In this verse, Allāh سُبْحَانَهُ وَتَعَالَىٰ clearly states that the faces will be glowing on a day and that this will be at a time in which they will be granted the vision of their Lord سُبْحَانَهُ وَتَعَالَىٰ.

*Second Evidence*

The second piece of evidence proving the possibility of seeing Allāh سُبْحَانَهُ وَتَعَالَىٰ from the Noble Qur'ān is the asking of Sayyidunā Mūsā عَلَيْهِ السَّلَام for it.

This desire expressed in the court of Allāh سُبْحَانَهُ وَتَعَالَىٰ by Sayyidunā Mūsā عَلَيْهِ السَّلَام is mentioned in the Qur'ān:

وَلَمَّا جَآءَ مُوسَىٰ لِمِيقَاتِنَا وَكَلَّمَهُۥ رَبُّهُۥ قَالَ رَبِّ أَرِنِيٓ أَنْظُرْ إِلَيْكَ

*"And when Mūsā arrived at our covenant and his Lord spoke to him, he said, 'My Lord, show me so I will look at You.'"* [63]

---

[62] *Sūrah al-Qiyāmah: 22-23*

[63] *Sūrah al-'A`rāf: 143*

Sayyidunā 'Imām 'Ibn al-Humām رَحِمَهُ ٱللَّهُ mentions this while listing proofs establishing the possibility of seeing Allāh سُبْحَانَهُۥ وَتَعَالَىٰ. He writes:[64]

ونفس سؤال موسى عليه السلام الرؤية إذ لا يسأل نبي كريم من أولي العزم الرب جل وعلا ما يستحيل عليه أ رأيت المعتزلي أعلم بالله سبحانه من نبيه موسى حيث علم ما يجب لله ويستحيل عليه ما لا يعلمه نبيه وكليمه عليه السلام

*"And the request of Mūsā, upon him be salutation, itself for the vision because a noble prophet from the 'ūlū al-`azm will not ask the Lord, the Majestic and Exalted, for what is impossible for Him. Do you think that the Mu`tazilī is more knowing about Allāh, glory be to Him, than His prophet Mūsā, such that he would know what is necessary and impossible for Allāh while His prophet and the one who spoke to Him, upon him be salutation, does not know?"*

## *Evidence From the Prophetic Narrations*

Besides the crystal-clear verses of the Noble Qur'ān establishing its possibility, much is found in the narrations of Sayyidunā Rasūl Allāh صَلَّى ٱللَّهُ عَلَيْهِ وَسَلَّمَ as well. One narration[65] of Sayyidunā Jarīr states:

---

[64] *al-Musāyarah: The First Section, Regarding the Dhāt of Allāh, the Exalted*

[65] *Saḥīḥ al-Bukhārī: Book of Tawḥīd, Chapter Regarding the Statement of Allāh, the Exalted, "The faces on that day will be glowing. To their Lord, looking.": 7436*

قال خرج علينا رسول الله صلى الله عليه وسلم ليلة البدر فقال إنكم سترون ربكم يوم القيامة كما ترون هذا لا تضامون في رويته

*"He said, 'The Messenger of Allāh exited unto us on the night of a full moon and said, 'Indeed, you will soon see your Lord on the day of resurrection as you all see this. You will not have to assemble in a crowd in His vision.''''*

This narration entails that the people will have no difficulty in seeing Allāh سُبْحَانَهُ وَتَعَالَىٰ, and just as there is no need to form a crowd to sight the moon, there will be no need to do so while seeing Allāh سُبْحَانَهُ وَتَعَالَىٰ.

Narrations similar to this one in meaning have been mentioned in *Jāmi` al-Tirmidhī* [66] and *Sunan 'Abī Dāwūd* [67] by Sayyidunā 'Abū Hurayrah رَضِيَ ٱللَّهُ عَنْهُ and in *Sunan 'Ibn Mājah* by Sayyidunā Sa`īd رَضِيَ ٱللَّهُ عَنْهُ.[68]

## *Evidence From Consensus*

The matter of possibility in seeing Allāh سُبْحَانَهُ وَتَعَالَىٰ is proven by consensus. Sayyidunā 'Imām Sa`d al-Dīn al-Taftāzānī رَحِمَهُ ٱللَّهُ states:

[66] *Jāmi` al-Tirmidhī: Book of Description of Paradise by Allāh's Messenger: 2554*

[67] *Sunan 'Abī Dāwūd: Book of the Sunnah, Chapter Regarding the Vision: 4730*

[68] *Sunan 'Ibn Mājah: Book of Introduction, Chapter of What the Jahmīyah Denied: 179*

وأما الإجماع فهو أن الأمة كانوا مجمعين على وقوع الرؤية في الآخرة وأن الآيات الواردة في ذلك محمولة على ظواهرها

*"As for the consensus: It is that the nation consensually agrees on occurrence of the vision in the hereafter and that the appearing verses regarding that are applied on their apparent meanings."* [69]

Furthermore, Sayf Allāh al-Maslūl, Sayyidunā 'Imām Faḍl al-Rasūl al-Badāyūnī رَحِمَهُ ٱللَّهُ writes:

ولا خلاف عندنا أنه تعالى يرى ذاته المقدسة وأن رؤيتنا له سبحانه جائزة عقلا في الدنيا والآخرة... واتفقوا أهل السنة في وقوعها في الآخرة واختلفوا في وقوعها في الدنيا

*"There is no dispute amongst us in that His Divine Entity will be seen and that our viewing of Him, glory be to Him, is logically possible in the world and the hereafter… The 'Ahl al-Sunnah agree on its occurrence in the hereafter and dispute in its occurrence in the world."* [70]

## *The Task of The Believer*

It may be difficult to grasp the idea of seeing Allāh سُبْحَانَهُ وَتَعَالَىٰ as He exists unbound by the constraints of space and direction, and that which we are accustomed to seeing is something which is in a particular direction and space. However, the responsibility of a Muslim is not to believe in only what he can comprehend. The believer is to believe in all that is said by Allāh سُبْحَانَهُ وَتَعَالَىٰ and His Messenger صَلَّى ٱللَّهُ عَلَيْهِ وَسَلَّمَ, and to leave what

[69] *Sharḥ al-`Aqā'id al-Nasafīyah, Chapter: The Vision*

[70] *al-Mu`taqad al-Muntaqad: Chapter of 'Ilāhīyāt*

concerns him to his Lord سُبْحَانَهُ وَتَعَالَىٰ and His Master صَلَّى ٱللَّٰهُ عَلَيْهِ وَسَلَّمَ.

'Imām 'Abū Ja`far al-Ṭaḥāwī رَحِمَهُ ٱللَّٰهُ, after the discussion of the divine vision, states:

فإنه ما سلم في دينه إلا من سلّم لله تعالى ولرسوله صلى الله عليه وسلم

وردّ ما اشتبه عليه إلى عالمه

*"Indeed, one is not safe in his religion except he who submits to Allāh, the Exalted, and to His Messenger, may Allāh send blessing upon him and salutation, and leaves what perplexes him to its knower."* [71]

## WAS THE VISION GRANTED ON THE JOURNEY OF MI`RĀJ?

There is a difference in opinion regarding whether the Messenger of Allāh صَلَّى ٱللَّٰهُ عَلَيْهِ وَسَلَّمَ was bestowed the divine vision on this blessed night of *Mi`rāj*. The overwhelming majority hold that the vision was indeed granted to him.

Sayyidunā 'Imām Faḍl al-Rasūl al-Badāyūnī رَحِمَهُ ٱللَّٰهُ writes:

قال صاحب الكنز قد صح وقوعها له صلى الله تعالى عليه وسلم

وهذا قول جمهور أهل السنة وهو الصحيح

*"The author of Kanz said, 'The occurrence of it is established for him, may Allāh send blessing upon him and salutation. This is the word of the majority of the 'Ahl al-Sunnah, and it is the accurate position.'"* [72]

---

[71] *al-`Aqīdah al-Ṭaḥāwīyah*

[72] *al-Mu`taqad al-Muntaqad: Chapter of 'Ilāhīyāt*

*Note:* The fact that there is a dispute in the occurrence is yet another proof of its possibility as the sensible would only dispute regarding something which is possible. If it was impossible to see Allāh سُبْحَانَهُ وَتَعَالَىٰ, there would be no conflict regarding its occurrence.[73]

The 'Imām of the *'Ahl al-Sunnah*, the reviver of 'Islām, the eradicator of innovation, Shaykh al-'Islām 'Imām 'Aḥmad Riḍā' رَحِمَهُ ٱللَّٰهُ, has given an extensive number of proofs establishing the occurrence of the vision on the night of *Mi`raj* in this pamphlet, *Munabbih al-Munyah li Wuṣūl al-Ḥabīb 'ilā al-`Arsh wa al-Ru'yah.*

In this pamphlet, the Genius Scholar of 'Islām رَحِمَهُ ٱللَّٰهُ has mentioned statements of Sayyidunā Rasūl Allāh صَلَّى ٱللَّٰهُ عَلَيْهِ وَسَلَّمَ, the Noble Companions, the *tabi`ūn*, and the Pious Predecessors رَضِيَ ٱللَّٰهُ عَنْهُمْ all in affirmation of the vision. Due to the excessive number of narrations included within the pamphlet, only a few of them will be mentioned.

## *Statements of Allāh's Messenger* صَلَّى ٱللَّٰهُ عَلَيْهِ وَسَلَّمَ

The Noble 'Imām 'Ahmad Riḍā' رَحِمَهُ ٱللَّٰهُ mentioned a total of four narrations which are directly attributed to the word of Sayyidunā Rasūl Allāh صَلَّى ٱللَّٰهُ عَلَيْهِ وَسَلَّمَ. Two of these narrations are to be mentioned.

---

73 *al-Bidāyah fī 'Uṣūl al-Dīn: The Statement of Possibility in Seeing Allāh, the Exalted*

'Imām 'Aḥmad رَحِمَهُ ٱللَّهُ, in his *musnad*, narrates from Sayyidunā `Abd Allāh bin `Abbās رَضِيَٱللَّهُعَنْهُمَا that the Messenger of Allāh صَلَّىٱللَّهُعَلَيْهِوَسَلَّمَ said:

رأيت ربي عز وجل

*"I saw my Lord, the Dominant and the Majestic."*

Both, 'Imām Jalāl al-Dīn al-Suyūṭī رَحِمَهُ ٱللَّهُ in *Khaṣā'iṣ Kubrā* and `Allāmah `Abd al-Ra'ūf رَحِمَهُ ٱللَّهُ in *Taysīr Sharḥ Jāmi` Ṣaghīr*, have stated that this narration is of an authentic chain of transmission.

The second narration is of 'Ibn Mardawīyah from Sayyidatunā 'Asmā' رَضِيَٱللَّهُعَنْهَا, the daughter of Sayyidunā 'Abū Bakr رَضِيَٱللَّهُعَنْهُ:

سمعت رسول الله صلى الله تعالى عليه وسلم وهو يصف سدرة المنتهى... قلت يا رسول الله ما رأيت عندها قال رأيته عندها يعني ربه

*"I heard the Messenger of Allāh while he was describing the Sidrah al-Muntahā… I said, 'O Messenger of Allāh, what did you see by it?' He said, 'I saw Him by it.' He means his Lord."*

## *The Statements of the Ṣaḥābah* رَضِيَٱللَّهُعَنْهُمْ

In this portion, 'Imām 'Aḥmad Riḍā' رَحِمَهُ ٱللَّهُ mentions six statements from the *ṣaḥābah* رَضِيَٱللَّهُعَنْهُمْ of which a few will be mentioned.

Tirmidhī reports from Sayyidunā `Abd Allāh ‘ibn `Abbās رَضِيَ ٱللَّٰهُ عَنْهُمَا:

أما نحن بنو هاشم فنقول إن محمدا رأى ربه مرتين

*"As for us, the Banū Hāshim, we say that surely Muḥammad saw his Lord twice."*

*Jāmi` al-Tirmidhī* and the *Mu`jam* of Ṭabrānī mention a narration from `Ikrimah, and the words of Ṭabrānī are as follows:

عن ابن عباس قال نظر محمد إلى ربه قال عكرمة فقلت لابن عباس نظر محمد إلى ربه قال نعم جعل الكلام لموسى والخلة لإبرٰهيم والنظر لمحمد صلى الله تعالى عليه وسلم

*"It is narrated from ‘Ibn `Abbās that he said, ‘Muḥammad looked to his Lord.’ `Ikrimah says, ‘So I said to ‘Ibn `Abbās, ‘Did Muḥammad look to his Lord?’ He said, ‘Yes. He made the conversing for Mūsā, the friendship for ‘Ibrāhīm, and the viewing for Muḥammad, may Allāh, the Exalted, send blessing upon him and salutation.’’’"*

‘Imām ‘Ibn Khuzaymah and ‘Imām Bazzār report from Sayyidunā ‘Anas bin Mālik رَضِيَ ٱللَّٰهُ عَنْهُ:

إن محمدا صلى الله تعالى عليه وسلم رأى ربه عز وجل

*"Indeed, Muḥammad, may Allāh, the Exalted, send blessing upon him and salutation, saw his Lord, the Dominant and the Majestic."*

The narration of Muḥammad bin ‘Isḥāq mentions the position of Sayyidunā ‘Abū Hurayrah رَضِيَ ٱللَّٰهُ عَنْهُ:

إن مروان سأل أبا هريرة رضي الله تعالى عنه

هل رأى محمد صلى الله تعالى عليه وسلم ربه فقال نعم

*"Indeed, Marwān asked 'Abū Hurayrah, may Allāh, the Exalted, be pleased with him, 'Did Muḥammad, may Allāh, the Exalted, send blessing upon him and salutation, see his Lord?' He responded, 'Yes.'"*

## *The Statements of the Tābi`ūn*

In this portion, the Noble *'Imām* mentions, in total, the positions of eight individuals amongst the *tābi`ūn*, and some of their statements will be recorded here.

The *Muṣannaf* of `Abd al-Razzāq narrates on the authority of Ma`mar regarding Sayyidunā Ḥasan Baṣrī رضي الله عنه that:

كان يحلف بالله لقد رأى محمد صلى الله تعالى عليه وسلم ربه

*"He used to swear by Allāh that Muḥammad, may Allāh, the Exalted, send blessing upon him and salutation, had seen his Lord."*

Sayyidunā 'Imām 'Aḥmad Riḍā' رحمه الله mentions for the position of affirming the divine vision to be that of Ka`b Aḥbār, 'Imām 'Ibn Shihāb Zuhrī, 'Imām Mujāhid, 'Imām `Ikrimah, 'Imām `Aṭā bin Rabāḥ, the teacher of 'Imām 'Abū Ḥanīfah, 'Imām Muslim bin Ṣabīḥ Kūfī, and all the students of Sayyidunā `Abd Allāh bin `Abbās رضي الله عنهما.

## *The Statements of Latter Authorities*

After mentioning the statements of the *tābi`ūn* رَضِيَ ٱللَّهُ عَنْهُمْ, the Noble 'Imām 'Aḥmad Riḍā' رَحِمَهُ ٱللَّهُ mentions the statements of latter authorities in the religion.

Naqqāsh mentions in his *tafsīr* regarding 'Imām 'Aḥmad bin Ḥanbal رَحِمَهُ ٱللَّهُ that:

قال أقول بحديث ابن عباس بعينه رأى ربه رأه رأه رأه حتى انقطع نفسه

*"He said, 'I express my position by the narration of 'Ibn `Abbās. With his eyes, he saw his Lord. He saw Him, he saw Him, he saw Him!' until his breath ran out."*

Quoting 'Imām Shihāb al-Khifājī رَحِمَهُ ٱللَّهُ in *Nasīm al-Riyāḍ*, 'Imām Nawawī رَحِمَهُ ٱللَّهُ in his commentary on *Ṣaḥīḥ Muslim*, and `Allāmah Muḥammad bin `Abd al-Bāqī رَحِمَهُ ٱللَّهُ in *Sharḥ Mawāhib*, the Noble 'Imām رَحِمَهُ ٱللَّهُ clarifies that the dominating and preferred position in this matter is that Sayyidunā Rasūl Allāh صَلَّى ٱللَّهُ عَلَيْهِ وَسَلَّمَ saw Allāh سُبْحَانَهُ وَتَعَالَىٰ with the eyes of his blessed head on the journey of *Mi`rāj*.

May Allāh reward the Noble 'Imām 'Aḥmad Riḍā' رَحِمَهُ ٱللَّهُ.

## *Response to Narrations Which Negate the Vision*

Though there exist narrations which negate that the vision has occurred, the principle that must be kept in mind is: the absence of knowledge does not equal absence of occurrence.

The fact that narrations of affirming occurrence exist and that this matter is not one that has any room for input by independent judgment, the narrations in affirmation will be given preference. This is because one will only speak in such a matter from confirmed information and not by one's own whim.

# Conclusion

The blessed journey of *Mi`rāj* is not just one miracle, it is the gathering of numerous miracles and virtues bestowed unto the Most Beloved Messenger صَلَّى ٱللَّٰهُ عَلَيْهِ وَسَلَّمَ by Allāh سُبْحَانَهُ وَتَعَالَىٰ.

The love showered upon His Beloved Messenger صَلَّى ٱللَّٰهُ عَلَيْهِ وَسَلَّمَ is unimaginable, and the virtues granted to him are not in the reach of anyone else amongst the creation.

Several discussions regarding this blessed journey are included in this work, and much more than what is included from amongst the wisdoms of this journey has been left out in an effort to keep the work concise.

May Allāh سُبْحَانَهُ وَتَعَالَىٰ allow us to remain amongst those who moisten their tongues by the remembrance of the Beloved صَلَّى ٱللَّٰهُ عَلَيْهِ وَسَلَّمَ.

Sayyidunā 'Imām 'Aḥmad Riḍā' رحمه الله states at the conclusion of his renowned *Qaṣīdah Mi`rājīyah*:

ثنائے سرکار ہے وظیفہ قبول سرکار ہے تمنا

نہ شاعری کی ہوس نہ پروا ردی تھی کیا کیسے قافیے تھے

*Praise of the Master is the task; acceptance of the Master is the desire*
*There is no desire of poetry nor any care, howsoever the post-rhyme word or rhyme may be connected*

# HONORIFICS

| | |
|---|---|
| صَلَّى ٱللَّٰهُ عَلَيْهِ وَسَلَّمَ | *ṣallallāhu `alayhi wa sallam* – used following the mention of the Messenger Muḥammad, translated as, "May Allāh bless him and upon him be peace." |
| عَلَيْهِ ٱلسَّلَامُ | *`alayhis-salām* – usually used following the mention of a prophet or messenger, translated as, "Peace be upon him." |
| عَلَيْهِمَا ٱلسَّلَامُ | *`alayhimas-salām* – usually used following the mention of two prophets or messengers, translated as, "Peace be upon them both." |
| عَلَيْهِمُ ٱلسَّلَامُ | *`alayhimus-salam* – usually used following the mention of three or more prophets or messengers, translated as, "Peace be upon them all." |
| رَضِيَ ٱللَّٰهُ عَنْهُ | *raḍiyallāhu `anhu* – usually used following the mention of a companion of the Messenger, translated as, "May Allāh be pleased with him." |
| رَضِيَ ٱللَّٰهُ عَنْهَا | *raḍiyallāhu `anhā* – usually used following the mention of a female companion of the Messenger, translated as, "May Allāh be pleased with her." |
| رَضِيَ ٱللَّٰهُ عَنْهُمَا | *raḍiyallāhu `anhumā* – usually used following the mention of two companions of the Messenger, translated as, "May Allāh be pleased with them both." |
| رَضِيَ ٱللَّٰهُ عَنْهُمْ | *raḍiyallāhu `anhum* – usually used following the mention of three or more companions of the Messenger, translated as, "May Allāh be pleased with them all." |

# TRANSLITERATION KEY

| Arabic Letter | Latin Character | Arabic Letter | Latin Character |
|---|---|---|---|
| ا أ ء | a | ط | ṭ |
| ب | b | ظ | ẓ |
| ت ة | t | ع | ` \| `a \| `i \| `u |
| ث | th | غ | gh |
| ج | j | ف | f |
| ح | ḥ | ق | q |
| خ | kh | ك | k |
| د | d | ل | l |
| ذ | dh | م | m |
| ر | r | ن | n |
| ز | z | و | w |
| س | s | ه | h |
| ش | sh | ي | y |
| ص | ṣ | إ | i |
| ض | ḍ | ـا \| ـي \| ـو | ū \| ī \| ā |

www.ingramcontent.com/pod-product-compliance
Ingram Content Group UK Ltd.
Pitfield, Milton Keynes, MK11 3LW, UK
UKHW040743060225
454761UK00001B/37